AS/A-LEVEL YEAR 1

STUDENT GUIDE

OCR

Sociology

Component 1

- Introducing socialisation, culture and identity

- Option 1: Families and relationships

Steve Chapman

PHILIP ALLAN FOR
HODDER
EDUCATION
AN HACHETTE UK COMPANY

Philip Allan, an imprint of Hodder Education, an Hachette UK company, Blenheim Court, George Street, Banbury, Oxfordshire OX16 5BH

Orders

Bookpoint Ltd, 130 Park Drive, Milton Park, Abingdon, Oxfordshire OX14 4SB

tel: 01235 827827

fax: 01235 400401

e-mail: education@bookpoint.co.uk

Lines are open 9.00 a.m.–5.00 p.m., Monday to Saturday, with a 24-hour message answering service. You can also order through the Hodder Education website: www.hoddereducation.co.uk

© Steve Chapman 2016

ISBN 978-1-4718-4347-1

First printed 2016

Impression number 5 4 3 2 1

Year 2020 2019 2018 2017 2016

This Guide has been written specifically to support students preparing for the OCR AS and A-level Sociology examinations. The content has been neither approved nor endorsed by OCR and remains the sole responsibility of the author.

Cover photo: thakala/Fotolia

Other photographs: p. 61, Paul Hebditch/Fotolia; p. 70, Fotolia; p. 77, MrSegui/Fotolia; p. 84, yanlev/Fotolia; p. 93, SakhanPhotography/Fotolia; p. 102, erichon/Fotolia

Typeset by Integra Software Services Pvt. Ltd., Pondicherry, India

Printed in Italy

Hachette UK's policy is to use papers that are natural, renewable and recyclable products and made from wood grown in sustainable forests. The logging and manufacturing processes are expected to conform to the environmental regulations of the country of origin.

Contents

Content Guidance

Introducing socialisation, culture and identity (Section A)

Option 1: Families and relationships (Section B)

Questions & Answers

The AS examination

The A-level examination

■ Getting the most from this book

Exam-style questions

Commentary on the questions

Tips on what you need to do to gain full marks, indicated by the icon **e**

Commentary on sample student answers

Find out how many marks each answer would be awarded in the exam and then read the comments (preceded by the icon **e**) following each student answer.

Sample student answers

Practise the questions, then look at the student answers that follow.

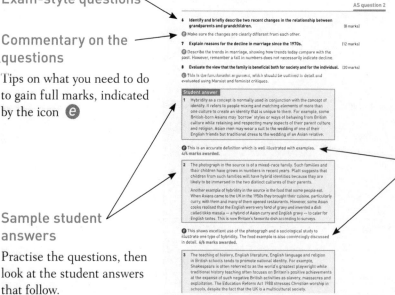

AS question 2

6 Identify and briefly describe two recent changes in the relationship between grandparents and grandchildren. [8 marks]

e Make sure the changes are clearly different from each other.

7 Explain reasons for the decline in marriage since the 1970s. [12 marks]

e Describe the trends in marriage, showing how trends today compare with the past. However, remember a fall in numbers does not necessarily indicate decline.

8 Evaluate the view that the family is beneficial both for society and for the individual. [20 marks]

e This is the functionalist argument, which should be outlined in detail and evaluated using Marxist and feminist critiques.

Student answer

1 Hybridity as a concept is normally used in conjunction with the concept of identity. It refers to people mixing and matching elements of more than one culture to create an identity that is unique to them. For example, some British-born Asians may 'borrow' styles or ways of behaving from British culture while retaining and respecting many aspects of their parent culture and religion. Asian men may wear a suit to the wedding of one of their English friends but traditional dress to the wedding of an Asian relative.

e This is an accurate definition which is well illustrated with examples. 4/4 marks awarded.

2 The photograph in the source is of a mixed-race family. Such families and their children have grown in numbers in recent years. Platt suggests that children from such families will have hybrid identities because they are likely to be immersed in the two distinct cultures of their parents.

Another example of hybridity in the source is the food that some people eat. When Asians came to the UK in the 1950s they brought their cuisine, particularly curry, with them and many of them opened restaurants. However, some Asian cooks realised that the English were very fond of gravy and invented a dish called tikka masala — a hybrid of Asian curry and English gravy — to cater for English tastes. This is now Britain's favourite dish according to surveys.

e This shows excellent use of the photograph and a sociological study to illustrate one type of hybridity. The food example is also convincingly discussed in detail. 6/6 marks awarded.

3 The teaching of history, English literature, English language and religion in British schools tends to promote national identity. For example, Shakespeare is often referred to as the world's greatest playwright while traditional history teaching often focuses on Britain's positive achievements at the expense of such negative British activities as slavery, massacres and exploitation. The Education Reform Act 1988 stresses Christian worship in schools, despite the fact that the UK is a multicultural society.

Component 1 **71**

■ About this book

This guide covers Component 1: Introducing socialisation, culture and identity as well as the option Families and relationships in the OCR Sociology specifications H180 (AS) and H580 (A-level). The content is identical for both, but A-level students will be expected to demonstrate a greater knowledge and understanding of sociological theory. The structure of the examination is also different for AS and A-level, so when you come to read through the questions, it is important that you note which are the correct ones for your course, though you may, of course, wish to use the others for revision or exam practice.

How to use the book

The first main section of the book is **Content Guidance**. It follows the headings for Introducing socialisation, culture and identity and the option Families and relationships in the OCR specification. Each part of the Content Guidance section contains exam tips, knowledge checks and definitions of some key terms. Knowing and understanding the meaning of sociological concepts is an essential part of the whole course.

The second main section of the book is **Questions and Answers**. At the beginning of this section are the three assessment objectives (AOs) against which your exam answers will be judged, with some guidance regarding how to display the required skills, and a list of command words, which will help you to understand more clearly what each question is asking you to do. The questions provided are in the style of the OCR exam for Component 1, and are divided into AS and A-level questions, each followed by an A-grade answer. Remember the importance of noting the structure and mark allocations of questions at the appropriate level for you, either AS or A-level. However, given that the content is the same, there is no harm in writing answers to all the questions given here — just remember when you look at the marks awarded and read the comments that they are being applied to a particular level, either AS or A-level. Throughout the student answers, you will find comments explaining why what has been written is good and is scoring well. More detailed guidance on how to use the Question and Answer section is given on pages 58–60.

Content Guidance

■ Introducing socialisation, culture and identity (Section A)

What is culture?

Culture, norms and values

Culture refers to the way of life of a society or social group which generally involves the learning and sharing of particular values, norms, beliefs, customs, language, history and knowledge. Giddens (1997) argues that it is culture rather than biology that makes people human.

Values are beliefs and goals relating to what members of a society or culture feel are morally important and desirable. They act as general guidelines for behaviour. The principal values of UK culture include respect for human life, free speech, achievement, equality of opportunity, materialism, individualism, fairness, justice and respect for privacy.

Norms are the cultural expectations or social rules that societies attach to particular types of behaviour. They often reflect key values. Norms affect all aspects of public and private behaviour, including diet, dress, romance, marriage, bringing up children, consumerism and so on. For example, in the UK, what, when and how we eat and drink, the ways in which males and females dress, how we express love, how we marry, how we treat our children, what we buy and so on are all shaped by dominant norms (and in turn by dominant values).

Both values and norms — and, therefore, culture — are relative concepts. This means that they are subject to change over time. For example, only 50 years ago, homosexuality was a criminal offence.

Customs are norms that have been established in a society for generations and are usually part of the historical traditions of a society that mark it out as culturally unique and distinctive. For example, in the UK Bonfire Night is celebrated on 5 November while in Wales, St David's Day is celebrated as a national festival on 1 March each year.

> **Exam tip**
>
> It is important to illustrate the relativity of both values and norms by using historical and cross-cultural examples.

> **Exam tip**
>
> When you revise, make a list of at least six norms and how they relate to key values.

> **Knowledge check 1**
>
> What value is promoted by the norms of knocking on people's doors to gain entry or not reading other people's diaries or letters?

Social roles are sets of norms or social rules which tell members of a society what should be the culturally expected behaviour of particular individuals. For example, the role of mother in the contemporary UK involves expectations about how 'good mothers' should behave, and is consequently used to socially judge individuals who may or may not live up to these expectations.

Status refers to the prestige or social standing attached to a particular role because members of a society or social group value highly the behaviour associated with that role. For example, doctors are held in high regard in UK society because their behaviour is directly concerned with saving lives.

Ascribed status refers to those roles that are fixed at birth by descent or inheritance, or by physical characteristics such as skin colour or gender. In some societies, the norms relating to the work people do, relationships, marriage, political and economic power and so on are restricted and unchangeable because status is ascribed. For example, the queen occupies an ascribed status because she inherited the position.

Achieved status refers to those roles which are achieved through education, qualifications, hard work, skill and talent. In Western societies such as the UK, roles and status tend to be achieved because members of such societies value equality of opportunity and merit. Lord Sugar is a good example of someone who has achieved his status, given his early beginnings as a market trader.

Types of culture

Subcultures are minority social groups that generally subscribe to the values and norms of mainstream culture but which also share values, practices, interests and problems that are unique to them.

Ethnic minorities living in the UK are subcultures because while they generally subscribe to the values and norms of most people in the UK, they may also subscribe to a daily religious and/or cultural lifestyle that reflects and celebrates their origins. However, subcultures are not restricted to ethnic minority or religious groups. Subcultures may originate in age differences. For example, territorial violent gangs found in inner-city areas and **spectacular youth subcultures** such as teddy boys, mods, skinheads, hippies, punks, goths and hipsters can be seen to constitute distinct subcultures.

Subcultures may also be based on political or alternative ideas. For example, anarchists, squatters, New Age travellers and those who live on communes are subcultures because they tend to be anti-authority or are in conflict with some aspect of mainstream culture (although that does not necessarily mean that they totally reject mainstream culture).

Finally, some sociologists suggest that the different lifestyles experienced by the working class, the middle classes and the upper class indicate the existence of class subcultures. For example, in some parts of the north of England, following rugby league is very much a working-class pursuit whereas following rugby union tends to be a middle-class pastime.

Exam tip

Make a list of social roles that you could use to illustrate this concept — for example, police officer.

Knowledge check 2

Is marriage an ascribed or achieved status?

Exam tip

You may be asked to compare and contrast youth subcultures. Make sure you know at least two in enough detail to do this.

Spectacular youth subcultures These tend to be composed of young people who are marginalised or disaffected by society in some way or who simply want to rebel or be different. They often develop a visible and strong sense of group identity which may be expressed in the form of everyday lifestyle, dress codes, taste in music, shocking or deviant behaviour and so on.

Think about how you might illustrate the concept of subcultures with reference to religion, language, dress codes, diet, leisure activities, alternative lifestyles etc.

High culture refers to the particular products and practices of a culture which are seen as intellectually and aesthetically superior because they supposedly represent the highest levels of human creativity. Such products include classical music and theatre, opera, literature and art, while high cultural practices might include enjoying ballet or reading poetry. It can also be applied to sporting activities — for example, polo, lacrosse, hunting and shooting.

Marxist sociologists are critical of high culture. For example, Bourdieu argued that high culture occupies the 'superior' position that it does because the capitalist class can use its economic and political power to impose its definitions of moral and artistic worth on the rest of society via the mass media and educational system.

Popular culture (sometimes called mass culture) refers to those cultural products and practices which do not aspire to higher intellectual or creative superiority and which are enjoyed and/or appreciated by the majority of ordinary people. Popular culture is often the product of the mass media and includes listening to pop music, watching television (especially soap operas and reality TV), going to the cinema and reading popular fiction (such as detective, horror, science fiction or romantic stories).

There is a sociological debate about the worth or value of popular culture.

- Supporters of high culture suggest that popular culture is inferior and often dismiss it as low culture. This is probably because a good deal of popular culture is mass-produced by global media companies for instant consumption by global audiences in order to make profit rather than art. Critics therefore tend to write it off as worthless because it has allegedly produced a dumbed-down entertainment and celebrity-obsessed consumer culture which encourages people to value materialism at the expense of critical and creative thinking.
- Marxist sociologists are critical of popular culture because they see it as a type of social control. Marxist critics such as Marcuse suggest that popular culture is used by the ruling class to encourage the population, especially the poor, to passively and uncritically accept the status quo and therefore inequality. Popular culture supposedly does this by celebrating celebrity and materialism. Marxists argue that popular culture fails to encourage the poor to ask serious critical questions about the way capitalist societies are organised. Inequalities in wealth and opportunity are consequently rarely questioned or challenged.
- Another perspective on popular culture is the **postmodern** approach, which suggests that it can no longer be classed as a mass culture. Strinati argues that there exists a wide variety and therefore massive choice of cultural products within popular culture.
  Many of these choices stimulate public critical debate about issues that are rarely discussed. These debates sometimes lead to important social change. For example, popular television soap operas such as *Eastenders* and *Hollyoaks* have encouraged

Marxism Marxists are critical of modern capitalist economies which they see as characterised by class inequality and conflict. They argue that a minority group — the bourgeois ruling class — has enriched itself by exploiting the labour power of the majority group — the proletariat or working class.

Be ready to illustrate the concept of popular culture with reference to television channels and programmes, sport and buying newspapers.

Postmodernism Postmodernists suggest that UK society has evolved from a modern industrial society into a postmodern post-industrial society in which consumerism, the mass media and globalisation now exert the most influence in shaping culture and society and, therefore, people's sense of identity.

public discussion of social problems whereas social networking media such as Twitter and Facebook may have made people more aware of particular issues and increased the pressure on politicians to deal with them.

Exam tip

Think about examples that might be found in a popular television soap opera or on social networking sites that might be used to illustrate this postmodernist point about popular culture.

Postmodernist writers also argue that the distinction between high and popular forms of culture is no longer clear cut because technology such as the internet has made all cultural products available to everyone. For example, people no longer have to leave their homes to visit an art gallery — many art treasures can be seen online. Moreover, postmodernists note that high culture and popular culture are increasingly being mixed and matched — for example, classic literature is adapted into popular television, classic art images adorn T-shirts, while television coverage of the football World Cup was sound-tracked by classical music.

Global culture refers to how the domestic cultures of societies like the UK can no longer exist in isolation from the rest of the world and are now influenced and shaped by **globalisation**.

The internet, social networking sites such as Twitter, Instagram and Facebook, satellite television, international monetary and stock market exchanges, multinational corporations such as McDonalds, Microsoft, Starbucks and Amazon, global political powers such as the European Union and NATO, and the cultural dominance of US music, film and television ensure that UK citizens are continually exposed to and perhaps influenced by worldwide events, trends and fashions. For example, many of the consumer brands available in British high streets and shopping centres are global in the sense that they are produced, advertised and sold by transnational or global companies.

Exam tip

It is important that you have a clear understanding of the meaning of globalisation and global culture and are able to illustrate these concepts with lots of economic and cultural examples.

Some sociologists predict that British and other national cultures will gradually be replaced by a global culture, shaped and controlled by global companies which will socialise world consumers into much the same identity as far as consumer needs and wants are concerned. However, it is argued by other sociologists that globalisation does not really exist in its purest form because most of these so-called global products are produced by the USA.

Consumer culture is a relatively recent phenomenon which has been fuelled by a rise in living standards, greater consumer choice of goods and the growing popularity of materialism. In consumer cultures, members of society increasingly value the pursuit of shopping as a major leisure activity. **Conspicuous consumption** is a common means of expressing identity in a consumer culture.

Globalisation This is the process by which societies across the world are increasingly connected and made interdependent by innovations in telecommunication and computer and information technologies as well as trends such as cheap air travel, mass tourism and migration. The world has become a smaller and more immediate place as a result.

Conspicuous consumption A person may express their identity and 'good taste' through the acquisition and consumption of so-called high status goods, that is, global designer-label brands such as Versace, Gucci or Ferrari.

There is evidence that consumer culture may be shaping values and norms. For example, credit card debt is a social norm today whereas only 30 years ago, being in any form of debt was seen by the majority as irresponsible.

Cultural diversity

Cultural diversity refers to cultural differences that exist in societies despite the fact that there is consensus or agreement on fundamental values and norms and that people still experience a common sense of belonging. For example, sexuality is a common aspect of cultural diversity. Sixty years ago, in the UK, being openly gay was a criminal offence and Britain was a fiercely heterosexual society. In 2015, gay subcultures freely exist in British cities such as Manchester and Brighton.

Cultural diversity is particularly visible in the neighbourhood make-up of British cities. Some ethnic minority groups have established themselves as distinct communities, such as the Chinatowns of London, Liverpool, Manchester and Glasgow, and the Bangladeshi community and the African-Caribbean community in the London areas of Brick Lane and Brixton respectively. Some areas, for example Luke Street in Liverpool or the East End of London, are well known for their working-class ties; Bloomsbury and Hampstead are famous for their middle-class connections; while Hoxton, Greenwich and Shoreditch in London are notorious for their hipster presence.

A multicultural culture or society is one in which ethnic and religious diversity is acknowledged and encouraged. Aspects of all cultures — majority and minority — are accepted and celebrated. The emphasis in multicultural societies is on all ethnic and religious subcultures enjoying the same status and rights, living alongside each other peacefully and respecting each other's beliefs, customs and heritage. A multicultural society, therefore, is one which celebrates difference, although critics of the concept suggest that the natural tendency of people from similar backgrounds to congregate together in distinct communities may encourage mutual suspicion, separation and even racial conflict.

Cultural hybridity

Cultural hybridity refers to how members of society, especially young people, are increasingly mixing and matching elements of the different cultures that now exist in the UK to construct a sense of identity. For example, white teenagers may be influenced by black and/or Asian culture in terms of clothing styles, hairstyles, body piercing, gestures of respect (the fist-bump, the high-five and so on), linguistic style and activities such as street dance, rap and hip-hop.

Another example of this hybridity can be seen in how British tastes in food have changed over the past 30 years. Foods from all over the world, especially pizza, lasagne, pasta and curry, have become popular in the UK. Many of these have been adapted to meet British tastes. Chicken tikka masala, which has replaced fish and chips as Britain's favourite dish, is a hybrid dish: Asian chefs based in the UK combined a spicy curry with the British concept of gravy to appeal to British palates.

Knowledge check 3

What role do the mass media play in the construction of personal identity according to postmodernist sociologists?

Summary

- Culture is the way of life of a society.
- Values, norms, customs and roles are important aspects of culture.
- Cultures are often diverse in nature, that is, made up of subcultures organised around ethnicity, religion, age, social class, and sexual and political affiliation.
- Cultures produce products which are classified as having creative value (high culture) or as having mass appeal and low value (popular culture).
- Home-grown culture is increasingly influenced by consumerism and globalisation.
- British culture is a multicultural one in which cultural hybridity is becoming the norm.

What is socialisation?

The nature versus nurture debate

The nature versus nurture debate refers to the academic argument between sociobiologists, who believe that human behaviour is largely the product of nature, particularly people's genetic or biological make-up, and sociologists, who argue that the society or social environment in which the individual lives is more important in nurturing and shaping behaviour. Sociobiology claims that people inherit characteristics such as intelligence, personality, gendered behaviour, aggressive tendencies and so on. In contrast, sociologists note that if this was the case then men and women would behave the same way in all societies. However, this is not the case — there are significant cultural variations across the world in gender behaviour. Sociologists therefore argue that this means gender is learned behaviour — it is the product of a nurturing or **socialisation** process which is specific to particular cultures and societies.

Studies of wild (or feral) and severely neglected children also demonstrate the importance of the socialisation process. These rare cases typically involve the child being starved of human contact in their formative years and consequently they lack the skills that other children learn from their constant contact with their parents. In other words, nature rather than nurture has been the most important influence on their lives.

Socialisation

Socialisation begins in childhood in the family, as the older generations (parents and grandparents) teach the next generation how to fit into society. This is known as primary socialisation. However, primary socialisation is supplemented by other secondary agencies of socialisation such as the education system and the media.

Functionalist sociologists believe that as a result of successful socialisation, most children grow up to be law-abiding citizens who generally conform to society's expectations, that is, they go to work, they get married, they treat other people with respect and so on.

Primary socialisation: the family

Primary socialisation is the initial socialisation into the culture of a particular society that takes place throughout childhood within the family group. As part of the child-rearing process, parents transmit the dominant cultural values and norms

Socialisation This refers to the ongoing, life-long process whereby individuals learn and internalise the common values, norms, customs and roles of a society.

Knowledge check 4

What do feral children lack that makes them less human than children brought up in families?

Functionalism
Functionalist sociologists believe that modern societies like the UK are characterised by social order because the majority have been successfully socialised into both value consensus, that is, fundamental agreement on how people should behave, and social integration, that is, a feeling of belonging to and identification with the same community.

that children need to learn in order to take their place in society. The functionalist sociologist Parsons described the family as a 'personality factory' because parents produce children with identities and social qualities that 'fit' the social expectations of the society to which they belong.

For example, parents often use rewards and punishments to help children learn a sense of right and wrong, and to encourage belief in values such as achievement. Parents also act as role models and consequently they may encourage their children to imitate their behaviour in order that they subscribe to moral codes, acceptable masculine or feminine behaviour and a work ethic, for example.

> **Exam tip**
>
> Male sure that you can illustrate these ideas with concepts such as conscience and that you are able to give examples of the qualities parents expect of their children, the rewards and punishments used by parents and specific examples of how parents might act as role models.

However, **New Right** sociologists argue that socialisation in modern society is becoming less effective as a result of increasing trends such as divorce and the absence of a father in many one-parent families. They suggest that the existence of social problems such as child abuse, youth suicide, antisocial behaviour, drug addiction and eating disorders is evidence that some families may damage children.

Interactionist sociologists argue that socialisation in families is a two-way process because it is a negotiated process. Parents also learn from their children. Moreover, socialisation is not a universal process shared in the same way by all. Rather, it is experienced in different ways because of the influence of social class, ethnicity, religion and so on.

According to Marxist and **feminist** sociologists, the function of socialisation in the family is to make sure that children grow up accepting inequality, hierarchy, exploitation and male dominance as natural facts of life. Socialisation is therefore about working-class children or girls learning conformity and subordination.

Secondary socialisation

There are several agents of secondary socialisation.

The education system

The education system is an influential agent of socialisation because children now spend about 14 years in schools and colleges. For pupils starting school in England in 2015 it is compulsory that they attend school (or be in some form of training) until they reach their eighteenth birthday.

Socialisation in schools involves pupils and students learning a formal subject or knowledge-based curriculum which is ultimately tested through examinations and rewarded with qualifications. However, in addition to this, Marxists argue that there exists a **hidden curriculum**.

New Right New Right sociologists believe that cultural processes such as socialisation are being undermined by the nanny state, the media and the peer group.

Interactionism Interactionist sociologists are interested in observing how different groups interact with one another and how they interpret one another's actions.

Feminism Feminist sociologists believe that modern societies like the UK are characterised by male dominance, or patriarchy. They note that gender inequality is a fact of modern life and is particularly visible in the worlds of politics, science, education, religion, mass media and family.

The hidden curriculum This is the way in which the organisation of knowledge and teaching as well as school rules and routines shape pupil attitudes and behaviour.

Marxists believe that this hidden curriculum has an **ideological** function which benefits the powerful because it produces pupils who conform to the demands of teachers and schooling in general, for example, they attend regularly, they obey school rules, they are prepared to learn and to be punctual. Moreover, the 'hidden' consequences of examinations, qualifications, setting and banding/streaming in terms of ability, school sports days, speech days, assemblies and so on might be that children learn that values and norms such as achievement, individualism, competition, respect for authority and hierarchy and acceptance of failure without complaint are essential components of becoming good adult workers and citizens.

> **Exam tip**
>
> Be able to illustrate the notion of the hidden curriculum by identifying the sorts of behaviour unconsciously encouraged by sports days and award ceremonies.

Whereas Marxists argue that the hidden curriculum and therefore socialisation in schools operates to produce conformity in people both as children and adults, functionalists, in contrast, believe that the hidden curriculum operates in a positive and beneficial fashion because socialisation by schools produces model pupils and model citizens.

However, the neo-Marxist Willis argues that pupils can successfully resist the influence of the hidden curriculum. The persistence of in-school problems such as classroom disruption, truancy, high rates of exclusion from school and anti-school subcultures, as well as wider social problems such as crime, riots, antisocial behaviour and industrial action such as strikes, suggests that the critics of the hidden curriculum may have exaggerated its influence.

Religion

Until the mid-twentieth century, the Christian religion in the UK was a key agent of socialisation because it injected certain social values with a sacred or religious quality. These values became the moral or ethical codes which people used as guidelines to shape their behaviour. For example, most people in the first half of the twentieth century believed it was morally right to marry and morally wrong to have sex before marriage, to live with someone outside of marriage, to commit adultery or to be gay.

The latter part of the twentieth century saw a major decline in belief in Christianity and church attendance. For example, it is estimated that less than 5% of Protestants in the UK attend church on a regular basis. This decline, which is known as **secularisation**, has prompted some sociologists, notably Bruce, to claim that religious socialisation is no longer influential today. Some sociologists claim that the mass media have replaced religion as a source of moral values.

However, despite secularisation, other sociologists argue that religion continues to be important in terms of being seen as an agent of socialisation in two main ways. First, not all religions are in decline in the UK. Religion is still central to many ethnic minority communities, while fundamentalist Christian religions such as Pentecostalism and sects such as the Jehovah's Witnesses are thriving.

Ideology According to Marxists, an ideology is a set of ideas which works on behalf of the wealthy to successfully persuade those at the bottom of society that society is organised in a fair way, that those who are economically successful deserve their rewards and that class inequality should therefore be accepted without complaint.

Knowledge check 5

Why do functionalists and Marxists disagree about the function of the hidden curriculum?

Knowledge check 6

Why do the problems and behaviours listed here challenge the ideological power of the hidden curriculum?

Secularisation This refers to the process whereby religious beliefs and thinking, practices and organisations have declined in social significance.

Second, Davie argues that religion is still a major agent of religious socialisation because millions of people in the UK believe in God and regard themselves as Christian. She argues that most people believe in God without seeing the need to belong to an organised religion and that people's moral values are still shaped by religious socialisation but in a less visible way than in the past.

Mass media

A number of sociologists have suggested that the mass media — television, films, pop music, newspapers, magazines and the internet, especially social networking sites such as Tumblr, Facebook, Twitter and Instagram — may have replaced religion in importance as a secondary agent of socialisation. It is argued that young people in particular are more likely to turn to the media in order to provide themselves with a design for living, to help them construct the identity they want to project to the world and to help them make sense of their daily experiences.

On the other hand, some media sociologists have expressed concern about the influence of media socialisation on the behaviour of young children. They suggest that casual violence and antisocial behaviour are increasing in society because of exposure to violent images on television, in films and in computer games, which impressionable children and adolescents are copying. Postman argues that television and the internet have blurred the distinction between childhood and adulthood because they have exposed children to images and information about sex, money, violence, death and other 'adult' matters from which they were previously sheltered. There is also concern about the amount of cyber-bullying that occurs on social networking sites and its negative effect on young people's self-esteem.

However, in criticism of some of these ideas, it is important to note that media sociologists have neither proved nor disproved the view that media socialisation is the sole cause of young people's use of violence or their antisocial tendencies.

The workplace

The experience of the workplace not only teaches workers skills but it also socialises them into the informal rules that underpin work, that is, the duties and obligations associated with the role and status of being a worker. For example, workers learn the discipline required to go to work for 8 hours on a daily basis, what is required to secure promotion from their employers, how to interact and work as a team with their fellow workers, how to behave appropriately in the workplace and so on. They may have to follow a dress code which confers on them a very distinct and visible identity. Workers may also acquire a strong or weak sense of social-class identity from the socialisation experience of the work they do. For example, working alongside others and experiencing the same dangers, routines and exploitation may produce a strong sense of and pride in working-class identity.

The peer group

A peer group is usually a group of people of similar age or status who are connected by friendship and/or similar experiences, who see each other regularly and who may influence one another in terms of behaviour, tastes and dress, for example. Peer groups may be organised formally, that is, they may work together as part of a team at

Exam tip

Consider religions other than Christianity and list the ways that they socialise their followers with regard to diet, dress codes, worship, prayer and so on.

Exam tip

Think about how you might evaluate the workplace as a socialisation agency by focusing on those workplaces in which it is difficult to be different — for example, footballers coming out as gay.

work or be members of the same society or club, or informally, that is, they may hang around together as friends or they may share similar tastes in music or fashion or they may run together as part of a street gang. Peer groups are often underpinned by social factors such as class, ethnicity and gender because they tend to be cultural comfort zones in that people prefer to hang around with people with similar cultural — social-class and ethnic — backgrounds. The saying 'birds of a feather flock together' is apt in this sense.

Peer groups generally encourage their members to conform to particular values and norms. They have an especially strong influence on young people because they are a major source of status for them. For example, boys may receive status from their male peer group for being tough or for messing around at school. Teenage membership of such groups can lead to conflict between them and their parents. **Peer pressure** expressed through membership of anti-school, delinquent and deviant subcultures may encourage young people to adopt values and norms in opposition to those of mainstream culture, such as truancy, drinking, drug-taking, shocking dress codes and rebellion, which means they may come into negative contact with teachers or the police. The consequences of rejecting such peer group pressure may be bullying and isolation.

Peer groups seem to be important in helping young people to establish an identity. They therefore function to help young people through the difficult period of adolescence in which they aspire to independence and more freedom. In this sense, then, belonging to a peer group may act as a rite of passage, that is, peer groups may assist the transition from childhood or youth to adulthood. Peer groups are robust in that friendship groups often survive well into adult life.

Formal and informal social control

Socialisation involves social control — once cultural values, norms and rules have been learned, they may need to be enforced through the use of positive sanctions (rewards) and negative sanctions (punishment). Social control, therefore, refers to the means by which society makes sure its members generally conform to the culture and the rules that they have learned during the socialisation process. Formal agencies of social control include the law, the police, the courts, the government and the military. Informal agencies of social control include the family, the peer group, the mass media, religion, the education system and the workplace.

Formal agencies of social control

Formal agencies of control such as the police and the judiciary have a great deal of power, known as authority, over ordinary citizens. Authority usually derives from rules which are written down in the form of laws. Most people consent to live by these rules and the consequences that result if they are broken.

The job of the police and the courts is to enforce the laws established by the government, usually through Acts of Parliament. Members of society generally accept these Acts because they have been put in place by politicians who have usually been democratically elected. Acts of Parliament that establish laws and punishments therefore supposedly reflect the will of the people. Moreover, another reason that the majority of citizens in a society consent to formal social control by agencies such as

Exam tip

You may be asked to compare the values and behaviour of two peer groups. Make sure you know enough detail to do this.

Peer pressure
Adolescents are often under pressure from their peer group to fit in with their friends. This may mean engaging in 'deviant' behaviour such as drug-taking, delinquency, under-age sex and gang activity in order to be accepted by others. For example, many street gangs insist that new members undergo 'initiation' tasks which may involve carrying out violence on others.

Knowledge check 7

Identify two benefits and two negative consequences of belonging to a peer group.

the police and judiciary is because they benefit from it. The whole point of a law is to protect law-abiding citizens and to maintain social order.

Exam tip

Make sure that you have revised a list of punishments that may exist in the UK or elsewhere for breaking the law.

Institutions such as schools, colleges and universities, as well as organisations which employ people, also use formal means of social control. For example, schools usually have written rules which all pupils and students are expected to follow with regard to behaviour, uniform, hair length and so on. They also have formal punishments such as detentions, suspension and exclusion for those who fail to abide by the rules. Similarly, organisations have written formal disciplinary procedures that employees must abide by. On the positive side, employees may be appraised to identify their strengths and value to the organisation. On the negative side, incompetency and other failures such as persistent lateness may invoke sanctions such as verbal and written warnings, and eventually dismissal.

Knowledge check 8

Give examples of ways in which formal agencies of social control might punish people for breaking laws or rules.

Informal agencies of social control

Informal control is that which is exercised without the use of written rules and codes of behaviour. It is usually exercised by people with influence but in a casual and unofficial way. It is usually invoked when a person or group disappoints or subverts the social expectations of behaviour. For example, children are expected to obey and/ or respect their parents and teachers. When they do not, an informal response might be to express disappointment with the child in order to elicit shame.

Families, specifically parents, have a range of informal social controls that they might use to shape children's behaviour. In order to positively encourage particular types of behaviour, parents may express pride, love and praise for their children and/ or materially reward them. In order to deter their children from behaving in deviant ways, they may punish them by denying them particular privileges.

Knowledge check 9

Give examples of ways in which parents might punish children.

Some sociologists argue that the mass media are a social control agency. Functionalists note that, by reporting crime and punishment, the mass media remind us what the rules (laws) of society are. They also define what counts as appropriate behaviour for men and women, young and old. For example, a woman who does not conform to media expectations about femininity may find herself defined as deviant, and **moral panics** may be used by the older generation to control the younger generation.

Other agencies that use informal controls might include religion, school and the workplace. Many religions use the notions of eternal reward (the prospect of heaven) and eternal punishment (damnation and hell) to keep their followers in line. In schools, teachers may reward hard-working students with praise and encouragement. They place those students in top sets and give them more one-to-one attention. However, they may informally punish other students who are not abiding by their standards by placing them in bottom sets. Finally, informal social controls may operate in the workplace in that an impressive performance may be rewarded with promotion and/or a rise in pay, while failure to meet particular targets may result in constant criticism and being regularly passed over for promotion.

Moral panic This refers to the mass media's ability to create anxiety among the general population through sensationalist and exaggerated reporting about a particular group and to present that group as a threat to society.

Summary

- There is a debate as to whether human behaviour is the outcome of biology or nature or whether it is the product of culture or nurture.
- Studies of feral children suggest that nurture or socialisation is what makes people human.
- The family is the key or primary agent of socialisation, although different sociological theories disagree about the social outcomes of this process.

- There are several secondary agents of socialisation, including education, especially the hidden curriculum, as well as religion, the mass media, the workplace and the peer group.
- There exist formal and informal social controls and agencies which function to ensure that members of a society obey the rules and generally conform to social expectations.

What is identity?

The concept of identity

Socialisation and social control are important processes because they result in the internalisation of society's expectations, rules and standards. The individual is thereby transformed into a social being whose identity, outlook, motivation and desires are shaped by the society to which they belong.

Personal identity is a concept which refers to the sense of self, that is, how people see or judge themselves in terms of their individuality and difference from others. People construct their unique sense of identity by adopting particular values, priorities, desires and moral outlooks and by choosing to look or to behave in particular ways.

Social identity refers to the social roles and statuses that society assigns to people. These may be family roles (e.g. father, mother, children), community roles (e.g. lovers, friends, associates, neighbours) or occupational roles. Each role a person performs has cultural expectations attached to it, that is, society expects that role to be performed to a particular standard. The successful or unsuccessful performance of social roles can impact on personal identity because it can reinforce positive or negative feelings of self-worth.

Collective identity refers to the process of identifying with a larger social group and experiencing a sense of belonging or community. Bradley identifies two types. A passive or ascribed identity is usually acquired involuntarily via birth and socialisation, while active identities are a matter of choice — people may choose to identify with a particular football team, a political cause, a spectacular youth subculture and so on.

Some postmodern sociologists claim that people are now rejecting traditional sources of identity, such as those shaped by social class and ethnicity, in favour of hybrid identities formed by choosing to mix and match styles and influences from a wide range of media and global sources. It is argued that young people are choosing to construct unique identities which celebrate globalisation, cultural diversity, consumerism and individuality. However, critics maintain that this argument is exaggerated and that the traditional influences on identity, such as ethnicity, religion, class, masculinity and femininity, are still influential today.

> **The self** This is an individual's subjective sense of his or her own identity.

> **Knowledge check 10**
>
> Explain why age, social class and ethnicity are examples of passive identity. Why can gender sometimes be an active as well as a passive identity?

Ethnicity and identity

Ethnicity is defined by Marsh and Keating as 'a sense of cultural awareness and identity within groups that share a common history or heritage'. Such groups may use their **ethnic identity** to construct notions of differences or boundaries between themselves and other ethnic groups, that is, to reinforce the notion of 'them' and 'us'.

The modern UK is a multicultural society and is made up of a variety of ethnic groups. For example, the 2011 Census showed that 80% of the UK population was white — the majority of these are British-born but a significant number were born outside of the UK in Ireland, Eastern Europe (especially Poland), France, the USA and Australia. It is important therefore to understand that the white majority includes a number of ethnic groups — for example, there are significant cultural differences between the English, the Polish and the Welsh. Note too that there may be some overlap between national and ethnic identity.

In 2011, 20% of the UK population identified with an ethnic group other than white British. The term 'ethnic minority' is normally used to refer to people who originated in the former British colonies of the Indian subcontinent, that is, people of Pakistani, Indian and Bangladeshi extraction, and the Caribbean. The majority of ethnic minorities living in the UK from these backgrounds are British-born and hold British nationality.

An ethnic identity can be seen to have particular social features:

- A common racial origin and skin colour
- A common language that is different from that spoken by the majority group
- A common historical experience — for example, slavery, colonialism and global migration to Britain in the 1950s
- Identification with their country of origin despite being second- or third-generation British born
- Similar religious beliefs and practices
- Common shared customs and traditions relating to dress, marriage and family life, community, diet and food preparation, music and so on
- A belief that they are set apart from others and that there are distinct social boundaries between the group to which they belong and others. This may express itself in the form of a sense of injustice or grievance because they feel that the majority group is discriminating against them or because they feel their cultural needs or heritage are being neglected or devalued compared with other ethnic groups. For example, Rhodes found that white voters in Burnley felt 'cultureless' because in comparison with ethnic minorities, they felt they were criticised and dismissed as racist if they tried to celebrate or display their white identity or culture.

Socialisation and ethnic identity

Ethnic identity is the product of socialisation in that from a very early age the identities and personalities of people are shaped by social or environmental influences such as their experience of the family, the education system, religion, the mass media, the peer group and the workplace.

Ethnic identity The sense of identity that derives from sharing common factors such as origin, language, history, heritage, religion and traditions.

Exam tip

It is important to be able to evaluate the concept of ethnic identity. For example, find out why the terms 'African-Caribbean' and 'Asian' disguise the fact that there are lots of different types of African-Caribbean and Asian identities.

The family

Ghuman (1999) outlined some of the family or primary socialisation practices found in many Asian families in the UK:

- Children are brought up to be obedient, and loyal to and respectful of their elders and community.
- Arranged marriage, based on negotiation with one's parents, is generally accepted by the majority of young people.
- Respect for religion is still considered to be important, particularly in Muslim families.
- The mother tongue is seen as crucial in maintaining links between generations and in the transmission of religious values. Children therefore tend to be bilingual, and are often able to use the mother language (e.g. Urdu, Punjabi, Gujarati and Hindi) and English interchangeably.
- There is a strong sense of obligation to the elderly and extended kin. For example, Dench et al. show the importance of the extended family for Bangladeshi families living in the East End of London.

Reynolds (2004) found African-Caribbean family life in the UK produced a strong transnational African-Caribbean identity among young people. Her research indicated that collective and individual pride in African-Caribbean culture and identity was achieved by maintaining close family ties with extended kin living in the Caribbean via Skyping, e-mail and so on and by offering family members mutual economic and social supports regardless of where they lived in the world. Consequently, the young people in Reynolds' study claimed that these family ties reinforced their African-Caribbean identity and compensated for what they saw as their marginalised and excluded status in British society.

Education

Studies of Indian and Chinese children indicate the importance of educational success to family and ethnic identity. However, there is also evidence that ethnic identity can be undermined by aspects of the hidden curriculum. For example, studies of curriculum content suggest that the knowledge taught in schools tends to be **ethnocentric**. The contribution of black or Asian culture to history, literature, science, mathematics and so on is either rendered largely invisible or reduced to special occasions such as 'Black History Month' or stereotypical topics such as slavery and civil rights.

Another aspect of the hidden curriculum is the expectations that teachers might have with regard to particular ethnic groups. Sewell argues that entrepreneurship or 'hustling', as well as masculinity, are regarded as more important than academic achievement by African-Caribbean boys. Consequently, British teachers have low expectations of African-Caribbeans, especially boys, and treat them more unfairly and harshly in the classroom. This may account for the fact that black boys are more likely than any other social group to be excluded from school.

Religion

Some schools are 'faith schools', that is, they have been set up by specific religious groups — Christian, Jewish, Muslim and so on — to promote an ethnic identity underpinned by religious values and practices. Most faith schools in Britain are

> **Exam tip**
>
> Use the family section of this book to work out which family type is linked to ethnicity and how this might influence the socialisation of children.

Ethnocentric Cultural bias caused by the assumption that one culture is superior to another. In the context of education, the curriculum may be ethnocentric because it reflects the history of the ethnic majority, that is, it is a white and Western version of history, literature, science and so on.

church schools (e.g. Church of England, Roman Catholic) and the rest (around 1%) are non-Christian (e.g. Jewish, Muslim, Hindu). These schools are supposed to follow official guidelines with regard to equal opportunities and the teaching of tolerance for others. However, fears have been expressed by Law that faith schools furnish children with narrow, intolerant, uncritical and often patriarchal ethnic identities which reject any other way of seeing the world and which promote intolerance of lifestyles defined by the school as morally wrong — for example, homosexuality.

There is a strong relationship between religion and ethnicity. For some ethnic minority groups, particularly Pakistani, Bangladeshi, Indian and Jewish groups, religion is probably the most influential agent of socialisation outside the family and consequently religious identity overlaps considerably with ethnic identity.

Islam has a strong impact on young Pakistani and Bangladeshi identity in terms of diet, worship, dress, behaviour and everyday routines and practices. Some sociologists such as Jacobson have suggested that some young Pakistanis see being Muslim as more important than being Pakistani or British. She suggests that this is a defensive identity which may compensate for the lack of power experienced by young Muslims.

The peer group

A concept that has become central to a sociological understanding of the influence of peer groups is the **cultural comfort zone**, which refers to the fact that people from similar social and ethnic backgrounds tend to cluster together in public spaces such as college social areas.

Sewell has used the concept of a 'cultural comfort zone' in his study of why some young black boys fail at school and get involved in gang cultures. He has suggested three reasons — the triple quandary — for this. First, he argues that black boys have to deal with a dominant mainstream culture that is fairly middle class, mainly white, focused on achieving academic success and which has low expectations about the ability of black boys. This school environment is generally experienced by black boys as outside of their comfort zone.

Second, Sewell argues that black boys are often anxious about how they are perceived by their peers rather than their parents because many of them come from one-parent families in which their fathers are absent. However, behaviour which is admired and encouraged in this comfort zone of friends is generally non-academic because conformity to school values is associated with 'acting white' or as feminine.

Third, the cultural comfort zone — the area in the school where those who are not academic hang out — helps to preserve and develop the boys' ethnic identity within a white majority or academic situation. The peer group develops coping strategies to help overcome the dominance of white culture in school, such as the adoption of a vernacular street language that is not understood by teachers, a street identity based on 'respect' which is partly shaped by hip-hop music and a consumer culture which sees designer clothing and 'bling' as more important than education. This cultural comfort zone helps compensate them for the strong sense of rejection that they feel because of the absence of their fathers, the low expectations of teachers, racism and so on. However, it also attracts negative attention from the authorities as conflicts between black boys focused on respect/lack of respect result in increasing gang violence.

Exam tip
Make sure you know at least two ways in which religion may help people express their ethnic identity.

Cultural comfort zone
The awareness of common interests or sameness, as well as the sense of community, means that young people feel most comfortable in the company of people from similar cultural backgrounds.

The mass media

Sociological evidence suggests that people who have little or no experience of living alongside ethnic minorities often rely on the media for information about them. If that coverage is generally negative, racist prejudices may develop. Moreover, the self-esteem and identity of ethnic minorities themselves can be partly shaped by how the media represent them.

However, the evidence suggests that ethnic minorities are generally represented in stereotyped and negative ways across a range of media content. Van Dijk conducted a content analysis of tens of thousands of news items and found that news representations of ethnic minorities disproportionately focused on them as criminal, as a threat to the majority in terms of immigration, as asylum seekers, as potential terrorists and as subscribing to 'abnormal' beliefs and practices such as forced marriages, honour killings, female genital mutilation and 'repressive' dress codes.

Some sociological studies have focused on the role of black music, specifically hip-hop and rap music, in developing and reinforcing black identity. Best and Kellner argue that rap music gives young black people the means by which they can communicate anger about racism, especially police harassment but also the economic and social deprivation experienced in black neighbourhoods. Rap and hip-hop are therefore a powerful source of black identity because they supply a voice for those excluded by mainstream society and celebrate pride in blackness. However, on the negative side, Best and Kellner argue that these musical genres also celebrate misogyny, violence, materialism and greed.

Ethnic minority identity and culture are also influenced by a range of media outlets in the UK which target minority groups, such as the BBC Asian digital network, satellite channels such as Star TV, Vox Africa and the Islam channel, commercial radio stations such as Sunrise, Panjab and Desi and newspapers such as *Eastern Eye* and *The Voice*. Parker and Song note that new media too are now much used by ethnic minority groups to preserve culture, as seen in the multitude of arranged marriage websites on which people can seek possible husbands and wives and which they can access via their laptops and smartphones.

The workplace

Some ethnic minorities can be found in high-status and high-earning jobs such as medicine but a disproportionate number, especially Pakistanis, Bangladeshis and Africans, are employed in low-skilled and minimum-wage work. Hudson et al. note that low-paid ethnic minority workers experience a range of discriminatory barriers which prevent them from improving their workplace position. They often experience bullying and harassment from unsupportive management and fellow white workers. Rao and Stevenson found that ethnic minorities felt that they had to work harder and longer than their white workmates in order to be considered for promotion or the same recognition.

Unemployment levels are also disproportionately high for ethnic minority groups compared with the white majority. Evidence suggests that unemployment can have significant long-term and negative effects on identity in terms of stress, depression, helplessness, loss of self-esteem and suicidal thoughts.

> **Exam tip**
>
> Think about how certain jobs in which ethnic minorities might be disproportionately found, such as in restaurants or pharmacy, may be linked to family influences.

Hybrid identities

There is some evidence that ethnic identities are evolving and that modern hybrid or dual forms of identity are developing among Britain's younger minority ethnic citizens. Charlotte Butler studied third-generation young British Muslim women and found that some chose to reflect their ascribed identity through the wearing of traditional dress, while others took on a more 'negotiated' identity, that is, they adopted Western ideas about education, careers and equality while retaining respect for traditional religious ideas about the role of women, say, with regard to arranged marriage.

Johal found that second- and third-generation young British Asians subscribed to a dual identity that he called 'Brasian'. He suggests they inherit an Asian identity which they predominantly use in their home environment. However, they also adopt a form of identity which Johal calls a 'white mask' which they use in public spaces such as school to interact and connect with their white peers. Similarly, Ghuman suggested that Hindu and Sikh girls compartmentalise aspects of their daily experience. He noted that they behave as obedient and respectful daughters, wearing the salwar kameez and speaking in Punjabi/Hindi, at home. However, at school they speak English to one another while engaging with teachers in much the same way as their white peers.

Modood, however, while acknowledging the appearance of hybrid identities among young Asians, notes that the overwhelming majority of young British Pakistanis and Bangladeshis subscribe to a traditional Asian identity. Most choose to organise their domestic and personal lives on the basis of the values of their parents — obligation, duty, community, honour and so on. Modood therefore argues that tradition is still the main shaper of the ethnic identity of young people, especially in Muslim communities.

Hybridity can also be seen to be emerging from the relationship between white and black people. Interracial marriage has increased considerably in the past 30 years and dual-heritage children are the fastest growing group of children in the UK.

Globalisation has also encouraged ethnic hybridity. Youth of all ethnic origins can be found in the global fast-food outlets of KFC, Nandos and McDonalds and in coffee shops such as Starbucks. The global popularity of cultural products focused on other ethnicities in films such as *Slumdog Millionaire* has brought other ethnic cultures into our living rooms. Interracial friendships and the global dominance of black musical genres such as rap/hip-hop and nu-soul have led to young white people borrowing from and playing with language and style which originate in black culture as they attempt to construct their own **hybrid identities**.

Nationality and identity

Nationality is a formal, legal category which derives from people belonging to a specific 'nation state', that is, a country recognised by other countries as exercising authority and power over a geographical territory. Nationality is usually accompanied by legal rights such as being able to carry a passport, legally marry or vote at a particular age. It also involves certain duties such as obeying the law of the land.

Knowledge check 11

Why might mixed-race children be regarded as having a hybrid ethnic identity?

Hybrid identities This is the idea that identity in a multicultural and globalised society no longer relies on one specific culture for its characteristics because people now mix and match aspects of personal style from a variety of ethnic and global sources.

National identity, however, is not the same thing as nationality. Rather, it is defined as the feeling of being part of a larger community, that is, a nation state, which gives the individual a sense of pride, purpose and meaning. This may be expressed through patriotic or nationalistic attitudes, feelings and behaviour — for example, by volunteering to fight for one's country in times of war or supporting the national football team.

Guibernau and Goldblatt claim that British identity is a fairly recent invention and that it is based on five central themes:

- Geography, particularly Britain's island status, which means that the British feel separate from the rest of Europe.
- Britain's Protestant religious status, which differentiated the UK from the mainly Catholic Europe.
- Wars, particularly against other European countries, which some see as forging uniquely British characteristics such as self-sacrifice, the stiff upper lip, perseverance, fair play and putting up with exceptional hardship.
- The British empire, which has supposedly resulted in the British seeing themselves as culturally superior.
- The royal family, which is seen by the mass media to be at the very heart of British identity. For example, Billington argues that the death of Diana, Princess of Wales in 1998 was perceived by the media as a national calamity because of the central role the monarchy plays in constructing British identity.

Skey notes how British identity is sometimes expressed by the sentiment that 'others', because of their appearance, traditions and ways of behaving, are threatening 'Britishness'. This is British identity expressed through victimhood, in which majority interests are seen as threatened by minorities. Garner agrees that national identity is often expressed in negative ways — for example, through concerns about immigration, multiculturalism, religious **fundamentalism**, the ghettoisation of ethnic minorities and the failure to conform to British cultural norms.

Socialisation and national identity

Billig argues that the British people are mainly socialised into a British identity through agencies such as education, the mass media and religion.

Education

The teaching of history, English literature and religion in British schools tends to promote national identity. In 2014, in reaction to a controversial Ofsted report that some schools in Birmingham were promoting Islamic values rather than British values, Michael Gove (then Secretary of State for Education) announced that all schools would be required to promote 'British values' such as respect for democracy and British law, individual liberty, religious tolerance and opposition to gender segregation, although critics such as Hand question how uniquely 'British' these values actually are.

Migrants to Britain hoping to gain British citizenship and permanent residence must score at least 75% on the Life in the UK test. This includes questions that focus on the values and principles that supposedly lie at the heart of being British.

National identity The feeling of being part of a larger community in the form of a nation and identifying with national symbols such as flags, institutions, brands, foods and rituals.

Fundamentalism A belief in the literal truth of holy texts and a subsequent desire to return to traditional values and practices.

Exam tip

Find a copy of the Life in the UK test on the internet so you can give examples of the specific questions it asks.

Mass media

Sindic argues that mass media such as newspapers gave people the opportunity to imagine themselves as members of the same national community, who share the same experiences despite the geographical distances that physically separate them.

Anderson suggests that the mass media encourage British identity in a variety of ways. First, they encourage people to identify with national symbols such as the royal family by taking a keen interest in their activities. The mass media generally approve of and defer to the monarchy and are critical of the notion of **republicanism**. Members of the royal family are therefore treated as celebrities by the media and their lives are closely scrutinised. Second, some sections of the media may encourage national identity by promoting anti-European attitudes. Third, the media talk up British achievements in global sporting events such as the Olympics, the World Cup, Grand Prix motor racing, and the Tour de France. International sporting events are reported by the mass media almost as quasi-wars against other nations.

Religion

Over 60% of people in the UK identify with various types of Protestantism. In times of national celebration, such as royal weddings, national ceremonies marking disasters or terrorist outrages and remembrance ceremonies in honour of the war dead, the Protestant religion plays a central role in the proceedings. In the courts, people swear on the Bible and the national anthem asks God to look after the queen.

The decline of British identity?

Sociologists such as Condor, as well as Kennedy and Danks, argue that British or English identity may be under threat in the twenty-first century for a number of reasons.

- Celtic identity, especially Scottish and Welsh, has always been a powerful source of identity in Scotland and Wales respectively, and has been given political and legal legitimacy in those parts of the UK in the form of a Scottish Parliament and a Welsh Assembly, which have the power to introduce legislation on a wide range of issues. 44.7% of Scots voted to leave the UK in the 2014 referendum.

  Surveys routinely show that people born in Wales, and particularly those who speak Welsh as their first language, see themselves as Welsh only. Welsh identity has been assisted by legislation aimed at protecting the Welsh language and culture, especially in the education system. The Welsh language is compulsory in Welsh schools up to year 11 despite the fact that it is only spoken by a minority of the Welsh population.

- It has been suggested by Condor that while groups such as the Welsh and Scots have developed a strong sense of identity underpinned by language, history, education, government and media, the English are experiencing an identity crisis. It is argued that many English people, especially those who see themselves as liberals, have been unwilling to adopt the symbols of English identity, such as the St George's Cross because of its long association with racist political parties and football hooliganism.

  However, some English people are proud to openly and stridently display their English national identity. These 'Little Englanders' according to Denscombe are

Republicanism A set of ideas that believes power should lie in the hands of the people via elections and which rejects the idea that some people, that is, kings and queens, are born to rule.

Knowledge check 12

Identify other aspects of Welsh identity apart from those mentioned.

critical of multiculturalism, immigration, Europe and equal opportunity policies. The evidence suggests that this group may be increasing in number. For example, the 2011 Census found that only 14% of whites identified themselves as purely British. In contrast, 64% saw themselves as 'purely English'.

■ Kennedy and Danks suggest that national identity is being undermined by globalisation, especially economic and cultural globalisation. It is argued that developments in satellite television, smartphones and the internet mean that people are exposed to and can access information and consumer products from all over the world.

British identity may be undermined by economic globalisation as British companies and products are taken over by foreign companies and British companies close down their factories in the UK and move production to cheaper developing countries. There are also concerns that US culture is taking over the British high street as companies such as McDonald's and Starbucks expand their British operations.

Cultural globalisation may also erode British identity. British people often spend their leisure time watching television programmes and films and listening to music produced for the global market. The use of global commodities such as Coca-Cola, Nike sportswear, the Apple iPhone and so on is widespread. Facebook, Twitter and Instagram are global networking sites. This means that there may be little difference in the leisure activities of youth living in the UK and youth living in the USA, Brazil, India and Japan.

However, Sindic does not agree that globalisation is undermining British national identity. First, he notes that globalisation has led to an increase in choice of global products but there is little sign that these are transcending national identity. For example, there is greater access to food and restaurants from a multitude of countries but they are still identified by their national origin — Chinese, Indian, Italian and so on. Second, Sindic notes that people often choose to use global technology such as the internet to express, maintain and strengthen their national identity, that is, to reinforce their difference from other nationalities. Third, data from large-scale surveys do not support the view that national identity is in decline. The 2007 Eurobarometer found that 88% of the UK's population felt attached to Britain.

Gender and identity

Sociologists distinguish between the concepts of 'sex' and 'gender'. The former refers to the biological or physical differences between males and females. This is normally straightforward although some people who are biologically male may feel female and vice versa. These people are known as 'transexuals' and may seek hormonal treatment and/or surgery to bring their bodies into synchronisation with their feelings of being male or female.

The concept of gender refers to the social expectations of behaviour that society attaches to each sex. In other words, it refers to how societies and cultures construct masculine and feminine identities to which people are expected to conform. These differ from society to society.

Knowledge check 13

What is the difference between sex and gender?

The UK is a **patriarchal** society and consequently there exists a **hegemonic ideology** about how males and females should behave with regard to everyday behaviour. For example, this ideology suggests that males and females should dress differently, carry out different domestic responsibilities and go into different occupations. It suggests that 'manly' behaviour involves being tough and aggressive, taking risks and so on while 'ladylike' behaviour involves being passive, demure and submissive, being concerned with physical appearance, being caring and so on. However, it is suggested that these traditional gender identities are now being challenged by new versions of femininities and masculinities.

New femininities

It is argued that young women today have been unshackled from the patriarchal past in two main ways. First, changes in the economy have led to the feminisation of labour and the subsequent emergence of women's modern status as capable, flexible and aspirational workers/professionals. They have allegedly been liberated from the domestic roles of mother and housewife. Wilkinson argues that females today have experienced a **'genderquake'** in attitude and aspiration compared with their mothers and grandmothers. Young women today are keen on acquiring educational qualifications that open doors to professional careers and which furnish them with the income and freedom to choose their own path, independent of males.

Second, it is suggested that the economic independence of young women today means that they are more likely to be making the most of choices in terms of consumption. For example, Kehily notes that young women are now more likely to be assertive, 'out there' individuals — ladettes — who are visibly having it all and doing it all in terms of the night-time economy — drinking, clubbing, having sex and so on.

Kehily argues that over the last 30 years women seem to have gone from having marginal and almost invisible identities because they mainly occupied domestic roles to having active and visible identities in the public spheres of education, work and leisure. However, she notes that hegemonic definitions of femininity still exist in that young women are still subjected to the patriarchal notion that slimness equals happiness and their bodies are still objectified by the male gaze. The decision to start a family is still most likely to impact negatively on a woman's economic position rather than a man's. Moreover, the opportunity to enjoy the new femininity with its emphasis on freedom and pleasure is not equally distributed as some poorer girls from working-class backgrounds are more at risk of early motherhood and social/economic exclusion, while Seidler (2006) notes that girls from Muslim backgrounds are still subject to hegemonic ideas about the female role rooted in culture and religion.

New masculinities

Kehily argues that the masculine role of men has also radically changed as the economic landscape has changed. Thirty years ago, masculinity was expressed through hard work, especially manual work, and providing the family wage. However, the decline of Britain's manufacturing base has led to widespread unemployment among males. Men can no longer automatically expect to be breadwinners and providers. Some sociologists, such as Mac an Ghaill, argue that this has led to a **crisis of masculinity** — men today no longer know what is expected of them. This has had two broad effects.

Patriarchal The idea that society is male dominated.

Hegemonic ideology With regard to masculinity and femininity, this refers to a set of dominant and traditional ideas, which the family and other agents of socialisation champion, about how males and females ought to behave.

'Genderquake' A seismic or extremely large change in women's attitudes which has occurred over one or two generations.

Crisis of masculinity The idea that men's perceptions of what a man is and how he ought to behave has been undermined by economic and social changes such as the decline in men's jobs and long-term unemployment. This may be driving social problems such as suicide, divorce and domestic violence.

First, it has led to social problems such as more suicide, mental illness, crime and domestic violence as men struggle to make sense of masculine identity today and attempt to assert their masculinity in traditional ways.

Second, it has led to some men attempting to redefine masculinity either by paying more attention to their bodies in terms of the consumption of body maintenance products such as membership of gyms, toiletries, cosmetics and clothing or by amplifying their domestic roles, especially with regard to spending more quality time with their children, sharing in childcare and even becoming full-time house husbands.

Socialisation and gender identity

Gender identity is the product of gender role socialisation in that from a very early age feminine and masculine identities are shaped by a combination of agencies of socialisation such as the family, the education system, religion, the mass media, the peer group and the workplace. Some parents may attempt to resist traditional expectations about feminine and masculine behaviour although this generally proves impossible because children are exposed to so many social influences with regard to gender.

The family

Most sociologists agree that the family is the main or primary agent in socialising children into gender roles. Gender socialisation begins the moment children are born. Once a child's sex has been identified they are subjected to gender stereotyping. For example, newborn babies will be given blankets and clothing which is gender specific in terms of colours, that is, pink for girls and blue for boys. Witt found that parents expected their babies to act differently according to their gender within 24 hours of their birth.

As the child grows, so parents dress their infants in gender-specific clothing and give them toys, storybooks and birthday cards deemed 'suitable' for their gender. Pomerleau et al. studied children's rooms and found that little girls' bedrooms tended to be disproportionately pink in design and were stocked with dolls and other manipulative toys whereas little boys' bedrooms were disproportionately blue in design while their toys were mainly sporty and vehicular.

Wood's observation of parents suggests that fathers demonstrate a more rigid set of gender expectations than mothers. For example, fathers were more likely to use physical smacking and harsh verbal rebukes on their infant sons whereas they perceived their daughters to be softer and consequently more sensitive to criticism and discipline. Fathers also held their daughters more than they did their sons. Girls therefore were subjected to more gentle treatment which continued well into adolescence.

Exam tip

As part of your revision notes, compile a list of the different ways in which parents treat boys and girls. In addition to what is in this section, add the language used by parents to describe boys and girls, examples of gender-specific toys and so on.

Martin found that parents expect sons to be involved in active and energetic modes of play while girls are encouraged by parents to involve themselves in passive play organised around appearance and dressing up. Fine found that parents expect and encourage boys to be strong at sport. Similarly, parents expect and encourage girls to be more emotional and talkative, which results in them having better verbal skills than boys.

Education

Miller and Church argue that some teachers reinforce gender stereotypes within the classroom. For example, teachers expect boys to be noisier than girls and are more likely to punish a noisy girl compared with a noisy boy. Teacher–pupil interaction, therefore, may result in children learning that girls are expected to be passive and compliant while boys are expected to be boisterous and assertive.

There is also evidence from Frosh et al. that male behaviour at school can be divided into two broad types. Some boys are academic and value both positive relationships with their teachers and working hard to achieve academic success. Other boys, who subscribe to hegemonic masculine values and norms such as being tough and confrontational, tend to reject academic study as feminine. These boys believe that status and respect are best obtained by engaging in laddish anti-school activities such as disrupting lessons. Moreover, they often bullied the more academic boys, who they described as soft and weak.

There is also evidence of similar divisions among girls in schools. Fuller notes these divisions are often based on social class and ethnicity. Middle-class white girls and ethnic minority girls were often committed to academic work and were strongly encouraged to be this way by their families. Working-class girls, on the other hand, often saw education as a stopgap before leaving school and taking up jobs in shops or service trades such as hairdressing. These girls would often adopt classroom behaviour which was very similar to that of non-academic boys, that is, disruptive, aggressive and loud behaviour that often focused on talking about issues such as boys and spending time on personal appearance rather than completing academic tasks.

Religion

The experience of boys and girls with regard to religion is likely to be a traditional patriarchal experience because adult males generally occupy dominant roles and females generally occupy subordinate roles in most world religions. For example, religious organisations tend to have male-only hierarchies and there are few religions in which women are allowed to lead worship and prayer. Moreover, some religions physically segregate the sexes during worship and exclude women if they are menstruating or have recently given birth.

The sacred texts of most religions largely feature the doings of male gods, prophets and so on, and are largely interpreted by men in ways that benefit them rather than women. Some fundamentalist Christian, Jewish and Muslim religions would like to see women's rights to equality with men reversed because they believe that a woman's place is in the home bringing up children.

Exam tip

Remember to evaluate by briefly discussing how these processes may also be influenced by social class, ethnicity and religion.

Exam tip

Make sure you are able to identify, explain and evaluate at least two ways in which education socialises children into masculine and feminine roles.

Exam tip

Remember to evaluate by showing how educational processes may also be influenced by social class and ethnicity.

The peer group

Children are very influenced by their peers. Szegedy-Maszak found that primary school children used gendered stereotypes to judge the behaviour of other pupils. Boys who expressed an interest in feminine activities would be exposed to peer group pressure which would make it very clear that such interest was inappropriate.

Studies of adolescent behaviour suggest that teenagers conform to traditional stereotypes about the sexes. Adler et al. found that the popularity of boys depended on active and achievable characteristics such as athleticism, coolness, toughness, social skills and success in cross-gender relationships, while the popularity of girls depended more on passive and ascribed characteristics such as physical appearance, social skills and academic success.

Peer groups may be involved in the negative policing of gender in that if a male or female fails to conform to the group's expectations about how a male or female should behave they may be bullied by the group. Bullying may take a number of forms. Males tend to bully by using violence or by name-calling, while Garandeau et al. found that girls use 'relational bullying', that is, they share with other girls (and boys) hurtful information about other girls via social networking sites such as Facebook or by using e-mail or texting.

> **Exam tip**
>
> Be aware that you can use material in other sections to explain and illustrate how peer groups help shape gender identity such as Sewell's work on cultural comfort zones and black boys.

The mass media

Johnson's research focused on how gender identity is reinforced through television advertising. She found that advertisements focused on boys contained language and images that emphasised traditional male traits such as action, competition, destruction and control while advertisements that targeted females contained language and images that emphasised attractiveness, emotion and nurturing.

Magazines aimed at younger women may objectify women's bodies and send out the patriarchal message that women should treat their bodies, particularly their weight and appearance, as a project that is constantly in need of improvement. According to Kilbourne, this media representation presents women as mannequins: tall and thin, often size zero, with long legs, perfect teeth and hair, and skin without a blemish in sight. This 'beauty ideal' makes an appearance in a variety of media. Orbach argues that the media perpetuate the idea that slimness equals success, health, happiness and popularity. She is therefore critical of the beauty ideal because it encourages young girls to be unhappy with their bodies, which may lead to eating disorders. Magazines aimed at young men may encourage them to sexually objectify women's bodies.

Some sociologists argue that a variety of media, especially Hollywood films and computer games, transmit the view that masculinity based on strength, aggression, competition and violence is a natural goal for boys to achieve. However, there are signs that media representations of masculinity are starting to embrace new forms

> **Knowledge check 14**
>
> How do the male and female peer groups differ in their reaction to those who fail to conform to their expectations?

of masculinity that celebrate fatherhood (the **new man**) and emotional vulnerability (the **metrosexual man**). Moreover, in the past 20 years, the media have also become more accepting of homosexuality, as major celebrities have come out and declared themselves to be gay.

The workplace

Billington et al. point out that many men see their masculine identity as centrally linked to being paid workers, that is, with having jobs and/or careers. Men's family roles and identities are also tied up with their occupational roles. The dominant view of masculinity includes the notion that men should be breadwinners who are responsible for the living standards of their families. However, as mentioned on page 26, sociologists such as Mac an Ghaill note that working-class men and boys may be experiencing a 'crisis of masculinity' because of the decline in male jobs.

Billington suggests that the main source of feminine identity is still the woman's role as mother despite the fact that the economy has become feminised and the majority of adult women go out to work. Hakim agrees and suggests that many women choose to be mothers and are happy for this role to be the primary source of their identity. However, this is contested by Wilkinson who argues that traditional notions of female identity are in the process of being abandoned. Sharpe too notes that feminine identity today is more likely to be focused on education, career, independence from men and consumption than on marriage and family.

Social class and identity

Identity is strongly bound up with employment and the workplace, and the income, status and lifestyle that arise out of it. There is evidence that class identity, which is based on people's occupation and the income (wage or salary) they receive, is a powerful influence on the social relationships people forge. For example, workplace peer groups are often the basis of social networks outside work. Generally, it is agreed that three broad social class groupings exist in the UK: the upper class, the middle classes and the working class.

Upper-class identity

This group is defined by its wealth rather than occupation. A key value is that economic power (wealth) is a source of opportunity, privilege and power over others, which is worth reproducing and protecting. Two subcultural groups can be observed within the upper class, which makes up about 7% of UK society.

There is a traditional upper class made up of members of the royal family, the aristocracy and members of families who made their fortunes from manufacturing or retail and who have acquired titles, such as the Sainsbury and Guinness families. Many members of this class have inherited wealth and consequently do not need to work for a salary or wage. Their status is ascribed rather than achieved.

The second rich subculture is known as the 'super-rich' and is composed of those who have made their fortunes through hard work (for example, Lord Sugar or Richard Branson) or talent (for example, David and Victoria Beckham). Their status, therefore, is achieved rather than ascribed. The super-rich are distinctive because of the media

New man A media term used to describe the emergence of men who are more in touch with their feminine side and happy to share tasks such as childcare.

Metrosexual man A media term used to describe a man who is meticulous about his grooming and appearance.

Knowledge check 15

What is the main source of feminine identity for most women according to Billington?

focus on them as celebrities — many of them are footballers and stars of film and music — and their liking for conspicuous consumption — lavish lifestyles — which is often minutely detailed by magazines such as *Hello* and *OK*. Sometimes the world of the super-rich overlaps with the world of the traditional upper class: Princes William and Harry, for example, are often portrayed by the media as happy to move between these two groups.

Middle-class identity

Sociologists largely agree that the middle classes are defined by the fact that they carry out non-manual work. Light argues that respectability and decency are important aspects of most middle-class forms of identity. The middle classes are also aspirational and consequently they value education highly, especially higher education. The notion of 'deferred gratification' is also important, that is, that studying or saving when setting out on their career path will bring about future benefits.

Savage argues that there are cultural differences between the middle-class fractions of professionals and managers in terms of attitudes, pursuits and identity — for example, professionals are more likely than managers to take an interest in the arts. Saunders also notes differences in the cultural values and therefore class identities between professionals employed in the private sector, such as accountants or managers, and those employed by the state, such as teachers or social workers. The former tend to be highly **individualistic** and focused on improving the standard of living of their family, while the latter tend to be more **altruistic** and community orientated.

Braverman argues that white-collar workers no longer subscribe to a middle-class identity because of radical changes in their workplace. New technology, restructuring and the introduction of working practices such as those found in call centres have resulted in the **deskilling** of such workers, which, according to Braverman, has led to a reduction in their pay and status. Marshall found that many white-collar workers see themselves as working class although their cultural lifestyles still differed from the traditional working class in key respects such as the area in which they lived, ownership of property and cars, where they holidayed and so on.

Working-class identity

Sociologists largely agree that the working classes are defined by skilled, semi-skilled and unskilled manual work. Until the late twentieth century, many working-class manual workers subscribed to a 'proletarian traditionalist' identity that had the following characteristics:

- They lived in tight-knit communities, close to their place of work, e.g. mining communities.
- They saw society in terms of 'them' and 'us' (i.e. workers versus bosses) and consequently had a strong awareness of and pride in their class position and identity.
- The extended family — parents and children, grandparents, cousins etc. — was important because it acted as a mutual support system offering economic, social and emotional supports.
- They were more likely to be found in rented property, especially council housing.

Individualism An idea that states that people should put their own and their family's interests before those of others.

Altruism Working primarily for the good of others rather than oneself.

Deskilling The process by which employers reduce the skills of the workforce in order to exert greater control over it.

Knowledge check 16

Identify three different types of middle-class identity.

- Gender roles were very traditional. The man was the breadwinner while his wife was the homemaker.
- Male children often followed their fathers into the same type of job.
- They had a strong sense of loyalty to their occupational peer group. This community was demonstrated in their membership of trade unions and working men's clubs, as well as their tendency to vote for the Labour Party, which was traditionally seen as the party that best represented their interests as manual workers.
- They subscribed to values based on 'immediate gratification', that is, they lived for the moment in terms of spending money for pleasure and consequently were less likely to save.

However, since the 1960s, there has been a major decline in manual work and in the numbers of proletarian traditionalist workers, as traditional industries such as coal-mining, shipbuilding, iron and steel production and factory work declined because of recession, lack of investment and globalisation. Consequently, the proletarian traditionalist identity has become less common.

Some sociologists argue that a new type of working-class identity has gradually become dominant. This class identity — known as the 'instrumental and privatised' working class — is more likely to be held by workers in the newer manufacturing industries and by self-employed skilled specialists such as electricians, builders, plumbers and engineers. Fiona Devine suggests that this type of worker sees work merely as a means to an end, that is, they work purely for instrumental reasons to improve their privatised home lives and standard of living. This group is no longer naturally hostile towards capitalism because they see capitalism as effective in raising their living standards. Members of this new working class therefore have no heightened sense of class injustice, community or political loyalty. Rather, they believe in individualism (i.e. putting themselves and their immediate families first) rather than collective action. They vote for whichever political party is most likely to protect or improve their individual and economic interests. They define themselves primarily through their families, their lifestyles, their respectability and standard of living rather than through their collective experience of the workplace.

> **Exam tip**
>
> The notion of social change can be a useful evaluative tool so be aware of how and why the new working class may be replacing the old working class.

Socialisation and class identity

Class identity is a complex affair because there is often a difference between objective and subjective views of social class. The government and other agencies use objective measurement devices such as the National Statistics Socio-economic Classification (NS-SEC) to categorise particular occupations into social-class positions based on skill level, income and how much control and autonomy workers have in the workplace. However, objective measurements sometimes collide with subjective perceptions of social class, that is, how workers define their class identity. For example, some managerial and professional workers who have been upwardly mobile from working-class backgrounds, and who are objectively middle class, may insist that they are working class.

The family and class identity

Scott argues that upper-class families strongly value intermarriage and extended kinship networks because these result in **social closure**. Furthermore, children from upper-class backgrounds are often socialised into a culture of privilege by their

> **Social closure**
> A practice which ensures that entry to a particular group is denied to those who are not born into it.

families and parents organised around a country-house lifestyle, conservative attitudes such as respect for tradition and hierarchy, strict etiquette or social rules which govern interaction, sponsorship of high culture and exclusive social and sporting pursuits such as shooting, fox hunting and polo. This common background and social superiority is reinforced by their parents' willingness to invest thousands of pounds a year in public boarding schools for their children.

Studies of middle-class families suggest that they are very child-centred and that parents often spend a great deal of economic capital on educational toys, books and technology, private tuition and on buying homes in areas with good schools. They can also pass on **cultural capital** to their children. They often have privileged access to **social capital** too.

Lareau found that working-class parents emphasised the 'natural growth' of their children —they did not cultivate their children's special talents. Instead they believed that as long as they provided their children with love, food and safety, their children would grow up to be healthy and well-rounded individuals.

Education and class identity

Upper-class children are mainly schooled in exclusive and expensive private schools (public schools), such as Eton, Harrow, Winchester and Rugby. Such schools socialise upper-class children into the values of conservatism, respect for tradition, nationalism and acceptance of authority and hierarchy as natural outcomes of superior breeding and upbringing. Public-school students are encouraged to see themselves as the elite. Scott argues that such schools teach upper-class children to be hostile towards values such as equality and justice.

Power found a strong relationship between middle-class pupils and educational achievement. Many of them were academically successful in both the state and private sectors. A university education was usually taken for granted by such pupils and their families.

However, Forsythe and Furlong's research found that the costs of higher education and the prospect of debt are putting bright working-class students off higher education despite Evans' findings that most working-class parents place a high value on education and generally encouraged their children to do well.

The media and class identity

Newman argues that mass media representations of social class tend to celebrate hierarchy and wealth. Those who benefit from these processes — the monarchy, the upper class and the very wealthy — generally receive a positive press as celebrities who are somehow deserving of their position. The UK mass media hardly ever portray the upper classes in a critical light, nor do they often draw any serious attention to inequalities in wealth and pay or to the over-representation of public-school products in positions of power.

Newman also argues that the tabloid media dedicate a great deal of their content to examining the lives of another section of the wealthy elite — celebrities and their lavish lifestyles. He notes that the media over-focuses on consumer items such as luxury cars, costly holiday spots and fashion accessories that only the wealthy can afford.

Cultural and social capital Cultural capital consists of values, beliefs, knowledge and language skills which benefit children in educational environments, while social capital refers to parents using their social contacts, confidence and communication skills to get the most out of education for their children.

McKendrick et al. studied a week's output of mainstream media in 2007 and concluded that the causes and consequences of poverty were rarely explored across the news, documentaries or drama. Moreover, dramas such as *Shameless* and documentaries like *Benefits Street* treat poverty as negative and the poor as entertainment. They also strongly imply that poverty is the fault of the individual or of a subculture which is feckless, workshy and happy to live off benefits and the proceeds of crime.

The peer group and class identity

The upper-class peer group is central to this schooling experience because as children become adults it functions outside schools as an **old-boy network**, which confers economic and cultural advantages on its members.

Willis claimed that working-class boys form anti-academic subcultures in schools as they reject learning aimed at achieving qualifications because they see education as irrelevant to their futures as factory workers. Membership of this peer group helps them cope with the boredom of the school day by furnishing them with opportunities to 'have a laugh'.

Hollingsworth and Williams interviewed middle-class children about their experience of school and subcultures. These pupils admitted that they looked down on working-class pupils and generally dismissed working-class behaviour as antisocial, aggressive and loud.

Class identity and social change

Postmodern sociologists argue that class has ceased to be the main shaper of identity. Instead they argue that class identity has fragmented into numerous separate identities. Gender, ethnicity, age, region and family role interact with consumption and media images to make up people's sense of identity today. This is shaped by people's consumption patterns — their use of style, brands and designer labels.

However, research by Savage suggests that these postmodern ideas may be exaggerated. His survey indicates that aspects of social class such as awareness of working-class community and respectability are still a significant source of identity for many manual workers. Moreover, members of a range of classes are aware of class differences and are happy to identify themselves using class categories.

Sexuality and identity

Homosexual and lesbian identity

In the UK, heterosexuality has been traditionally defined as the dominant and ideal form of sexual identity because of its links to reproduction. In contrast, homosexuality was seen in the early part of the twentieth century as a form of deviant or abnormal sexuality. It was illegal and was punishable by prison.

However, in the 1950s, cultural attitudes towards homosexuality began to shift, and homosexual acts between consenting adults over the age of 21 years were decriminalised in the 1960s. By the 1970s, homosexuality was no longer defined as a psychiatric condition by doctors. In the 1990s and 2000s the age of consent for gay people was lowered to 16 and gay marriage was made legal in 2014. Gay people today are openly and proudly part of society, particularly in the arts. There were 32 openly

Old-boy network The informal network of contacts, supports and services provided in adulthood by ex-public schoolboys for one another.

Knowledge check 17

What is the main source of identity today according to postmodernism?

gay MPs in 2015. However, it is still difficult for sportspeople such as footballers and rugby players to come out as gay. These social changes support Weeks' view that sexuality is the product of culture rather than biology.

By the 1970s, a distinct gay subculture could be seen to have emerged in British culture. Rich suggests that the eventual emergence of gay and lesbian subcultures is remarkable considering that Western societies tend to be characterised by a fierce **compulsory heterosexuality**. Hegemonic masculinity states that 'real men' are not homosexuals. The mass media constantly subject people to heterosexual images through films, television programmes and advertising. Religious organisations criticise homosexuality as sinful, wicked and immoral. Homosexuality is rarely portrayed as a normal or ideal condition.

Much of the gay subculture that emerged from the 1970s focused on leisure and consumption — the 'pink pound' or spending power of gay professionals was targeted by gay bars, clubs and restaurants. At the same time, gay culture became politicised as gays sought to assert their identity. Furthermore, in cities such as London, Brighton and Manchester, Gay Pride marches sought to increase the visibility and social acceptability of gay people. Gay marriage was legalised in 2014.

These strategies, aided by the increasing number of celebrities coming out as gay, have made it easier for gay people to lead a normal life today, although it should also be acknowledged that prejudice and discrimination have not disappeared. Homophobic attacks on gay people are still relatively common and suggest that this type of sexuality is not accepted by all sections of the community.

Heterosexuality and identity

Heterosexuality too is the product of culture rather than biology. This can be illustrated by examining the way that definitions of sexual attraction have changed over the course of the last 100 years or so in Western societies. Studies of eighteenth- and nineteenth-century paintings suggest that the ideal of feminine beauty in this period stressed plump women, while even in the 1950s, female sexual icons such as Marilyn Monroe were much bigger women than the waif-like supermodels and celebrities favoured by the fashion industry and championed by the media today.

Another clue that suggests that heterosexuality is socially constructed rather than being the product of biology is the **double standard** that exists with regard to comparable male and female sexual behaviour. There exists an assumption that males and females have different sexual identities. Males are supposed to be promiscuous predators (they supposedly want to have sex with as many women as possible), whereas females are supposed to be passive and more interested in love than sex. Because of this, women's sexual identity carries risks. Lees found that women may be subjected to being negatively labelled a 'slag' or a 'slapper' by both men and other women if they appear to behave in similar sexual ways to men.

Disability and identity

Traditionally the identity of disabled individuals has been constructed either by medical professionals or by the mass media. The biomedical model of health has been dominant in its insistence that the identity of disabled people is shaped by their physical or mental impairments and that consequently they are unable to lead a

---

Compulsory heterosexuality The idea that society is constantly bombarded with heterosexual images because this is regarded as the 'right' sexual lifestyle to adopt.

Knowledge check 18

Identify four pieces of evidence that suggest that gay identities are more acceptable today.

Exam tip

The material on gender identity (pages 25–30) is mainly focused on heterosexuality and therefore can be used to answer questions on heterosexual identity.

The double standard The notion that it is socially acceptable for a man to have multiple sexual partners but unacceptable for women to behave in the same way.

'normal' life, that is, like that of the able bodied, and are dependent on their families and doctors for everyday care. Moreover, this view of the identity of disabled people sees their situation as tragic — they are seen as deserving of able-bodied society's pity and charity. The mass media play a big role in this — for example, by organising telethons such as Children in Need.

However, disabled sociologists such as Shakespeare and Barnes are critical of this view of disability. They see the identity of disabled people as a social construction. This means disabled people are disabled by society, particularly by the negative attitudes and stereotypes held by able-bodied people about disabled people. These prejudices, which are known as **disablism**, create social barriers that discriminate against people with disabilities and prevent them from leading independent lives. This can be illustrated in several ways:

- Mass media representations of disability are often negative. For example, research has found that disabled people tend to be represented on television as objects of pity or charity. Media representations rarely present such individuals as 'people who just happen to have a disability'.
- The built environment (e.g. toilets, access to buildings and transport systems) is often not suitable for the needs of disabled people, although this is improving.
- Employers are reluctant to employ disabled people, who are six times more likely to be refused job interviews. As a result, people with disabilities are more likely than able-bodied people to be excluded from well-paid jobs and to be economically disadvantaged. It is a fact that disabled members of society are more likely to be unemployed, to be lower paid if in a job and to be in poverty.
- There is evidence of widespread bullying of disabled people, that is, 'hate crimes' in both care homes and in wider society. In 2011 there were 1,788 recorded incidents of disability hate crime in the UK. Eight in ten disabled children, especially those with learning disorders, have been bullied in the UK.

Disablism The idea that the identity of people with disabilities is not shaped by physical or mental impairment but instead by society's prejudices and discriminatory practices.

Goffman argues that prejudice and discrimination against people with disabilities can have a significant effect on their identity and self-esteem. It can result in the 'disabled identity' becoming a master status in the eyes of both able-bodied and disabled people. A **self-fulfilling prophecy** can result — people with disabilities internalise and start to believe in the negative labels. This may produce dependency. Scott found this when he researched blind people — they had learned to depend on sighted people.

Self-fulfilling prophecy The idea that people's behaviour is shaped or caused by the labels imposed on them by society.

Disabled sociologists argue that more positive disabled identities should be promoted, stressing independence, choice and autonomy for disabled people. They believe that the state should invest in a disability-friendly social environment and should address prejudice and discrimination against disabled people.

Age and identity

The UK segregates its members by age. Consequently, the ways in which young and old people are treated have a significant influence on their identity.

Biology and age

Biology influences the way that society divides people by age. Babies, infants and children are not physically or psychologically developed enough to perform adult tasks, while the ageing process may mean that elderly people are not as physically or as mentally effective as they were when they were younger. However, sociologists point out that there are enough cultural differences across societies and even across subcultural groups within the UK to suggest that age differences are also socially or culturally constructed.

The social and cultural construction of age identity

In many traditional societies, people often do not know their birth date (meaning they do not celebrate birthdays) or precise age because births are not registered. Generally, people's age identities go through three major stages in traditional societies:

1   Children — they are regarded as dependent on older groups for protection and survival.

2   Adults — children go through a rite of passage or initiation ceremony, usually at puberty, in which they are instructed in adult ways. Boys may learn how to be warriors or hunters and have to endure several tests of skill and/or strength. Girls are also instructed on sexual matters so that they can become wives and mothers shortly after puberty. Both boys and girls therefore move from childhood straight into adulthood.

3   Elders — as people age in tribal societies, they often acquire greater status and power because they are regarded as having greater experience and wisdom than those who are younger.

In contrast, in modern Western societies such as the UK, the state insists that all births are registered. It is taken for granted that people know their birth dates and that they celebrate birthdays.

Bradley identified five major **generational** stages of age identity in the UK.

Stage 1: Childhood

This is regarded as a special, innocent and vulnerable time in which children should be cosseted and protected by their parents. They are supported in this enterprise by the state, which has introduced laws in order to regulate the quality of parenting. The state has also introduced legislation to create guidelines on what is acceptable behaviour for children. For example, schooling is compulsory between the ages of 5 and 18, and 10 is the lowest age at which a child can be held responsible for a criminal offence.

Stage 2: Adolescence or youth

This is the period between puberty and the achievement of full adult status, i.e. the teenage years. Entrance to adulthood in the UK is usually celebrated on the eighteenth birthday because this is the age at which the state confers legal adulthood via the right to vote, marry or leave home without parental consent or sit on a jury.

Before the Second World War, adolescence was regarded as part of adulthood, because the majority of youth left school in their early teens and started work. They were not recognised as a separate social category because they were indistinguishable from their parents in terms of values, tastes, behaviour and dress, for example.

The postwar period saw the emergence of a youth culture based on specific teenage fashions, hairstyles and tastes in music such as rock and roll, which the older

Generations
Generations are age groups that live through the same historical and social events, and whose common identity and attitudes are reinforced by similar experiences of consuming cultural goods such as fashion, music, films and television programmes.

generation found shocking and threatening. This culture was the product of an increase in young people's spending power, brought about by full employment in the 1950s. Business reacted to this lucrative new market by developing products specifically for young people, such as comics and magazines for teenagers, pop music, radio stations, transistor radios, fashion and cosmetics.

Contemporary studies of the mass media's portrayal of spectacular youth subcultures, particularly Thornton and Savage, suggest that teenagers are condemned more frequently than they are praised by the mass media. However, studies of young people suggest that the generation gap implied by media moral panics is exaggerated. There is little evidence that youth identity is significantly different in terms of what young people value compared with their parents. Most young people are generally conformist — they get on well with their parents and place a high value on traditional goals such as getting married, having children and buying a house.

Knowledge check 19

What is a moral panic?

Stage 3: Young adulthood

This stage of age identity is focused on the period between leaving the parental home and middle age. Wallace suggested that modern societies like the UK have private and public 'markers' which signify the beginning of adult identity. For example, private markers might include a first sexual encounter or first cigarette, while public markers include the right to vote or the approval of a bank loan. Hockey and James saw young adulthood as bound up with having freedom and independence from parents, control over material resources and responsibilities. It may also including making the decision to move out of the parental home, to cohabit, to get engaged, to get married, to have children and so on. It usually marks the end of formal education and the decision to commit oneself to a particular career path.

Stage 4: Middle age

There is some disagreement as to when middle age begins. Brookes-Gunn and Kirsch set it as low as 35 years, while others have suggested it might be as high as 50. Physical indicators of middle age include greying hair, the appearance of 'middle-aged spread' and the menopause in women. Social indicators include children leaving home for university and more money for leisure pursuits. There may also be emotional or psychological indicators, i.e. the mid-life crisis.

Stage 5: Old age

In the UK people have tended to retire in their 60s and consequently this decade of a person's life has been seen as the start of old age. However, Pilcher argues that because of increasing life expectancy and differences in generational attitudes, tastes and behaviour, we should differentiate between the 'young old' (aged 65–74), the 'middle-aged old' (aged 75–84) and the 'old old' (aged 85+).

In contrast to traditional societies, elderly people in the UK are not accorded much respect or status, because work is the major source of status in industrial societies. Loss of work due to retirement can result in a significant decline in self-esteem, social contacts and income, as well as a consequent rise in loneliness, poverty, depression and poor health in general. The low status associated with elderly identity in UK society is compounded by the fact that people are often stereotyped and discriminated against because of their age. This is known as **ageism**, and is expressed in three ways:

Ageism Prejudice and discrimination based on negative stereotypes about specific age groups. It is particularly a problem for elderly people.

■ It is often institutionalised — it may be embedded in overt and covert organisational and legal practices — although ageism has been officially outlawed by the 2010 Equality Act. Bradley noted that old people may be seen as less suitable for employment because they are assumed to be 'physically slow, lacking in dynamism and not very adaptable to change'.

■ It is often expressed through stereotypical prejudices underpinning everyday interaction with elderly people, which assume that a person's competency is limited by their age, i.e. they are too old to carry out a particular task. Pilcher noted that old people are often described in derogatory or condescending ways, especially in mass media representations of youth and old age. Advertising reinforces the view that the appearance of youth is central to looking good and that ageing should be resisted at all costs. Media and popular stereotypes tend to marginalise old people as inferior.

■ It assumes that the very old are vulnerable and dependent on younger and fitter adults for care and protection. Ginn and Arber noted that the increasing number of elderly people — in 2015, people aged 60 and over formed a larger part of the population than children aged under 16 — has led to fears about the associated costs to society, e.g. the rising costs of pensions and of the increased use of health and welfare services. This has resulted in media reports portraying elderly people as a 'burden' on taxpayers.

Note that the ways in which particular age groups or generations are treated are often shaped by influences such as gender, social class and ethnicity. For example, the experience of being an elderly African-Caribbean woman or elderly Asian man may be qualitatively different from that of being a white, middle-class, elderly man.

Knowledge check 20

What is ageism?

Exam tip

Be able to illustrate how each age stage is created and reinforced by socialisation by the family, education, peer group, religion, media and the workplace.

Summary

■ There are a number of different influences on identity, including notions of individuality and difference, social roles, social class, gender, ethnicity, globalisation and consumerism.

■ The UK is a multicultural society and therefore ethnic identities are important in their own right and as a source of hybrid identities.

■ National or British identity may be under threat from the resurgence of Celtic identities and globalisation.

■ Gender identities are evolving as society becomes less patriarchal and consequently new forms of masculine and feminine identities are appearing.

■ There are a number of distinct social-class identities but there is a debate as to whether these are in decline or not.

■ Identity may also be shaped for some by disability or society's reaction to it, as well as by age and ageism.

■ Option 1: Families and relationships (Section B)

How diverse are modern families?

Functionalism and the family

Sociological debate about the family was for many years dominated by functionalist theory. Functionalists believe that modern societies such as the UK are characterised by social order rather than chaos and therefore aim to explain this social stability. Most functionalists agree that society is a social system made up of a collection of interdependent social institutions such as the family, education, politics, the economy, the mass media and religion.

Functionalists believe that the social system functions to bring about and reinforce social order by socialising society's members into **value consensus** and by promoting **social integration**. As part of the social system, the family is seen as crucial to these social processes.

Four major themes can be seen in functionalist thinking about the family:

■ Functionalists see the **nuclear family** as universal — it exists in almost every known society — therefore, they suggest it is the most ideal form of family.

■ Parsons argued that the nuclear family functions for the greater good of society because it makes a massive contribution to the maintenance of social order, stability and social integration. It does this by performing key functions such as physically reproducing the next generation and economically supporting that generation until it reaches adulthood. It is also the key agent of primary socialisation, that is, it socialises children into the key values and norms of society, thereby promoting both consensus and a sense of citizenship, and ensuring that children aspire to take their place as workers and consumers in the economic system when they reach adulthood.

■ Functionalists argue that the family functions for the benefit of the individuals who comprise it because both adults and children profit from the emotional wellbeing and satisfaction associated with marriage and family life. In particular, Parsons argued that the family functioned to stabilise the adult personality by reducing the tensions brought about by the competitive nature of industrial society. It does this by promoting the concept of home and children as an antidote to the stresses and strains of modern life. In addition, the nuclear family also functions to provide social support, community, identity and security.

■ Functionalist ideas about the superiority of the nuclear family have led to the emergence of an 'ideology of the nuclear family' (sometimes called 'familial ideology' or 'familism'). This ideology, which has recently been adopted by New Right sociologists, suggests that other types of family are somehow inferior to the nuclear family ideal.

In the UK, functionalism was influential in shaping the work of Young and Wilmott, who identified a type of nuclear family that they called the **symmetrical family** as

Value consensus Value consensus refers to common agreement on and sharing of values.

Social integration Social integration refers to a sense of community or belonging to a society.

Nuclear family A family composed of two heterosexual married parents plus children who share a common residence.

Symmetrical family A type of nuclear family which features equality between the spouses.

dominating British family life from the 1970s. Young and Wilmott suggest that up to the 1960s working-class family life in Britain was organised along extended lines. Their empirical research conducted in the 1950s in the Bethnal Green area of the East End of London showed that **extended families** existed in large numbers in this period.

However, after the 1960s, these types of families went into decline because working-class communities were re-housed in new towns and on council estates after extensive slum clearance. Also, the welfare state and full employment of the 1950s undermined the need for a **mutual economic support system**. Bright working-class young men and women also made the most of educational opportunities and moved away from traditional working-class areas and consequently experienced less frequent contact with kin.

According to Young and Wilmott, the extended family unit was replaced by the symmetrical nuclear family, that is:

- 'privatised' — the family has infrequent contact with extended kin and neighbours
- 'dual career' — both husband and wife work
- 'egalitarian' — men and women have more economic equality and share domestic tasks, decision making and leisure time
- 'home-centred' — the family spends much of its leisure time in the home

Young and Wilmott claim that this type of nuclear family is now dominant in both middle-class and working-class communities across the UK.

The critique of functionalism

Despite the nuclear family's dominance, the functionalist view of it has come under attack for a number of reasons. First, some critics suggest that the functions of the nuclear family are not as important as they once were because secondary agents of socialisation such as the mass media and adolescent and adult peer groups are more influential over family members in the twenty-first century than parents and families.

Second, interpretivist sociologists argue that children are portrayed as overly passive with regard to the socialisation process. They are viewed as empty vessels being filled with culture by their parents. In contrast, interpretivists argue that children are active conscious beings who often influence and shape their parents' actions. For example, they may influence their parents' taste in fashion, music, television viewing and use of social media sites.

Third, functionalists fail to consider the idea that family life might be harmful rather than beneficial for individuals. For example, studies of the dark side of family life suggest that, on average, nearly four children a week die at the hands of their parents in the UK and that child abuse is a major social problem in the UK. Radford et al. in a study carried out on behalf of the NSPCC found that 1 in 20 children had been sexually abused in the UK while 1 in 14 children in the UK had been physically abused. Most of the abusers were members of the child's family rather than strangers.

Exam tip

It is important to achieve a theoretical overview of the family. Examiners are keen for you to demonstrate how different perspectives view the family.

Extended family
Extended families are usually composed of three generations of kin who share a common residence, that is, they live under the same roof or they see and support one another on a frequent basis because they all live in close proximity.

Mutual economic support system This refers to how working-class communities would support their members in terms of jobs, money, babysitting, caring for the sick and so on.

Knowledge check 21

Why did the symmetrical family replace the extended family according to Young and Wilmott?

Marxism and the family

Marxists argue that the nuclear family benefits the wealthy and politically powerful capitalist class at the expense of the working class and the poor. Similarly, feminists reject the functionalist view that the nuclear family generally benefits society and all family members. They suggest that the nuclear family benefits men at the expense of women.

Marxists such as Zaretsky claim that the modern nuclear family benefits capitalism and the capitalist class at the expense of other members of society in three ways:

- It socialises children into an ideology which promotes obedience, conformity, showing respect for hierarchy and those in authority and so on. Consequently, such children grow up to become conformist citizens and passive workers who accept inequality and exploitation as part of the 'natural' state of things.
- Zaretsky argues that the nuclear family's function is to help workers manage their resentment of the capitalist workplace, which generally oppresses and exploits them. It does this by promoting the idea that workers should not engage in actions that threaten the standard of living of the family unit. Consequently, workers who are married with children may be reluctant to engage in industrial action, which ultimately benefits those who run that system.
- Zaretsky argues that capitalism is dependent on consumerism and that the nuclear family, as a major unit of consumption, is essential to the success and profitability of the capitalist system. He argues that parents are encouraged to teach their children that the main route to happiness and status lies in consumerism and the acquisition of material possessions. Consequently, the inequalities in wealth and income produced by capitalism often go unchallenged by a generation fixated on the acquisition of the latest designer labels and gadgets.

Marxists are probably correct in their observation that the nuclear family is deliberately targeted by advertisers as a unit of consumption and that the family is essential to the health of the capitalist economy. However, they fail to consider that some working-class parents may resist ruling-class ideology by teaching their children values and norms which are the product of working-class culture and which empower their children with knowledge of capitalist inequality and exploitation. Zaretsky also may be guilty of ignoring the very real emotional and social satisfaction that people get from being members of a family.

> **Exam tip**
>
> A useful way to evaluate is by juxtaposition, that is, to compare one theory of the family with another.

Feminism and the family

Feminists are highly critical of the functionalist theory of the nuclear family. They believe that the nuclear family has harmful effects for women and that it is generally responsible for patriarchy and the inequalities that patriarchy generates between men and women.

Marxist-feminists such as Ansley focus on the **dark side of family life**. She argues that male workers are often frustrated and alienated by the experience of work because the way work is organised in capitalist societies denies men satisfaction and power. This

Dark side of family life
This refers to the social problems that are found in some families, such as violence and abuse.

frustration is absorbed by the family, particularly the female partner, because men attempt to assert power, control and authority in the home to compensate. This often takes the form of domestic violence and child abuse. Wives and families, therefore, act as safety valves for capitalism because these men are not directing their anger at the real cause of their problems — the nature and organisation of capitalism.

In contrast, radical feminists believe that patriarchy benefits all men regardless of their wealth and status and that patriarchy and gender inequality originate in the nuclear family because women's dependence on men derives from their childbearing and child-rearing functions. Moreover, children are taught patriarchal ideology, especially the idea that the sexual division of labour is 'natural' and unchangeable via gender-role socialisation. Radical feminists such as Redfern and Aune have examined why the nuclear family is often the site of violence against women and children. They argue that such violence is the product of patriarchal ideas which see women as second-class citizens and which are deeply rooted in a society's history and culture. The family is the means by which that patriarchal history and culture is reinforced and transmitted to the next generation.

Many radical feminists believe that the patriarchal nuclear family must be abolished and alternative ways of living such as female-only communes must be encouraged. Firestone, for example, argues that women should use new reproductive technologies (e.g. in vitro fertilisation or IVF) to exclude men from families, while Greer argues in favour of **matrifocal families** in which power is in the hands of wives and mothers.

Liberal feminists agree that the family is a patriarchal institution which mainly benefits men but argue that positive progress is being made towards egalitarian families. They point out that changes in family law mean that women now have the same family rights as men. The availability of the contraceptive pill on the NHS means that women now exercise control over when to have children and how many to have. Young women are taking advantage of both education and the feminisation of the workforce to establish careers. Women who are unhappy with their marriages are using divorce to escape them. There is also evidence that, compared with previous generations, men are carrying out more domestic labour and childcare. However, liberal feminists do acknowledge that egalitarian family relationships will take at least another generation to be truly established.

The New Right and the family

New Right sociologists believe that the nuclear family is under attack or threatened by government social policies. These commentators often assume that there was once a 'golden age' of the family, in which husbands and wives were strongly committed to each other for life, and children were brought up to respect their parents and social institutions such as the law. New Right views on the family therefore reflect a dominant **familial ideology**.

Many New Right thinkers see the emergence of feminism and government social policies in the 1960s and early 1970s as the beginning of a sustained attack on traditional family values. They are therefore critical of several government social policies such as the legalisation of abortion, the introduction of laws promoting equal opportunity and family rights for gay people, equal rights for women in the workplace,

Matrifocal families
Families in which women are the head of the household.

Exam tip

In all essay questions which contain reference to a theory or debate, remember that once you have described the theory or view which is the focus of the question, you must consider alternatives.

Knowledge check 22

What is happening to the role of women in families according to liberal feminists?

Familial ideology A set of ideas which suggests that the nuclear family is the ideal that all families should strive to emulate.

the availability of the contraceptive pill on the NHS, the reform of the divorce laws and the availability of state welfare benefits, particularly for single mothers.

The New Right have also been critical of more recent government social policy. They claim that the New Labour government of 1997–2010 devalued the nuclear family by constructing a 'nanny state' which interfered too much in family life. Morgan claims that Labour's family policy undermined marriage and the nuclear family because it was biased in favour of single parents, cohabitation, dual-career families and gay people. The coalition government of 2010–15 was also criticised by the New Right for failing to strengthen marriage and family life, and especially in its failure to deal with family breakdown.

Trends in marriage, cohabitation and divorce

Marriage

In 1972, a record number of 480,000 couples in the UK were married. However, since then, the annual number of marriages in England and Wales has gone into steep decline. In 2009, a record low of only 231,490 couples got married, although since then the number of marriages has increased slightly. The mean age at first marriage in 1972 was 24.9 for men and 22.9 for women. However, the last 40 years have seen a significant rise in the age at which people are getting married for the first time. In 2012, the average age had increased to 32.4 for male first marriage and 30.3 for female first marriage.

The New Right identify three main reasons for the decline in marriage. First, Rector claims that the benefits system encourages single parenthood at the expense of married parenthood because it reduces the financial need for marriage. Second, the New Right argue that secularisation — the decline of religious belief and practice, especially among Christians — means that marriage vows are no longer sacred and traditional ideas such as life-long commitment in marriage are now seen as old fashioned and redundant. Third, the New Right claim that cohabitation is increasingly seen as an alternative to marriage.

However, feminist thinkers argue that the decline in marriage rates that the UK has experienced over the past 40 years reflects a positive change in the nature of marriage. There are four strands to this feminist argument.

- Marriage only appears to be in decline because men and women are delaying it because it is now regarded as the primary rite of passage — the most important decision in a person's life — that requires great emotional commitment.
- British Social Attitude (BSA) surveys indicate that most people, whether single, divorced or cohabiting, still see marriage as the most desirable life-goal, that is, the gold standard of relationships.
- Around 40% of all marriages are remarriages, which suggests that marriage is still popular as a social institution despite people's previous negative experience of a specific marriage.
- The decline of marriage has been exaggerated by the New Right. In 2012, 67% of families in the UK were headed by a married couple and at any one time approximately 21 million people in the UK are married. The majority of women in the UK (84%) are married by their fortieth birthday.

Knowledge check 23

Why is the nuclear family in decline according to New Right sociologists?

Exam tip

Try to learn the names of sociologists who have conducted research. When you cite them in an essay, this means you are referencing sociological evidence for which you will be rewarded.

Cohabitation

Cohabitation is defined by the Office for National Statistics (ONS) as living with a partner, but not married to or in a civil partnership with them. Cohabitation is one of the fastest-growing household types in the UK. The number of couples living together outside of marriage has doubled since 1996. In 2012, there were just over 2.9 million opposite-sex cohabiting couples and 69,000 same-sex couples. Moreover, in 1938, only 4% of babies in the UK were born outside marriage but in 2012 this had risen to 47.5%.

New Right sociologists such as Morgan claim that cohabitation is less stable than marriage. She refers to cohabitation as 'marriage-lite', claiming evidence that suggests that cohabiting couples are less happy and less fulfilled than married couples, more likely to be abusive, unfaithful, stressed and depressed and therefore more likely to split up.

However, Beaujouan and Ni Bhrolchain's study of cohabitation is generally critical of this New Right position:

- Cohabitation has become a normal part of the life course in the UK — about two-thirds of people aged 25–44 have cohabited at some point in their lives. Cohabitation, therefore, is no longer seen as socially deviant or immoral.
- Beaujouan and Ni Bhrolchain argue that cohabitation has strengthened marriage because it is seen by most couples as a test of compatibility, that is, a trial run for marriage. They argue that cohabitation may be responsible for the decline in marriages ending in divorce by their fifth anniversary because it 'screens out' weaker relationships that without cohabitation might have immediately progressed to marriage.
- They point out that cohabitation might be necessary for practical reasons, that is, because people are awaiting divorce or because weddings are expensive.

Divorce

Divorce refers to the legal ending of a marriage. Before the Divorce Reform Act of 1969, one partner had to prove the 'fault' or 'guilt' of the other for matrimonial 'offences' such as adultery, desertion or cruelty in order to obtain a divorce. This was usually very costly and complex because it involved a trial with a judge, barristers and so on. Consequently, divorce rates were low. However, the Divorce Reform Act changed the legal rules for divorce in a fairly radical way. From 1971, couples could obtain a divorce on the grounds of irretrievable (that is, permanent) breakdown once they had completed the legal formality of 2 years of agreed separation or 5 years of separation if one spouse objects to the divorce. This is a cheaper option and does not involve the need for a public hearing.

'Quickie' divorces are still available under the old rules, in that one spouse can sue the other on the grounds of adultery or unreasonable behaviour. This type of divorce still involves going before a judge and proving fault. It is therefore an expensive option. Since 1984, couples have been able to petition for divorce after the first anniversary of their marriage, that is, the legal separation can begin 12 months after the wedding.

In 1938, only 6,000 divorces were granted in the UK but this figure had increased tenfold by 1970 to 58, 239. The 1969 Act led to a dramatic increase in divorce. In 1993, the number of divorces peaked at 165,000. However, the general trend in

Exam tip

Remember all marking is positive. You will not be penalised if you make a mistake.

divorce between 1994 and 2012 has been downwards, with only 118,140 divorces in 2012. Nevertheless, New Right sociologists have expressed concern that successive governments have not done enough to prevent the breakdown of marriage and the consequent increase in the number of one-parent families.

There are a number of reasons for the rise in divorce after 1971. First, it is likely that many couples who had been in empty-shell marriages, or who could not afford to divorce after separating, took the opportunity of the new legal rules in 1971 to escape from their unhappy marriages. Second, functionalist sociologists argue that high divorce rates are evidence that marriage is more valued today and that people are demanding higher standards of marital behaviour in terms of emotional and sexual compatibility and equality in decision making and domestic tasks from their partners.

Third, feminists suggest women expect far more from marriage than men and may be using divorce to escape particular marriages when their husbands fail to live up to their high expectations. The fact that 54% of women-initiated divorces in 2012 were on the grounds of the husband's unreasonable behaviour supports this feminist perspective. Moreover, many women have careers and are no longer economically dependent on men. They no longer have to remain involuntarily in empty-shell marriages.

Exam tip

Examiners are quite keen on postmodernism. Make sure you know this theory well.

The postmodernists, Beck and Beck-Gernsheim, argue that increasing divorce rates are the product of a rapidly changing and postmodern world in which the traditional rules, rituals and traditions of love, romance and relationships no longer apply. They argue that the postmodern world is characterised by three important social influences:

- individualisation — people are less constrained by society and have consequently become more selfish
- conflict — marriage has the potential to become a battleground in which the selflessness required by marriage clashes with individualism
- choice — people in postmodern societies have a greater range of choices available to them in terms of lifestyle and living arrangements. In the postmodern world, divorce may merely be regarded as another lifestyle choice

Knowledge check 24

Identify four reasons why divorce has increased since 1972.

Demographic changes and family life

The study of demography is focused on how the number of births and deaths, and the number of people entering and leaving the country (migration), all affect the size, sex and age structure of the population. Sociologists argue that demographic changes over the past 100 years have had a major influence on British family life and in particular have contributed to the rich diversity of family types and living arrangements found in the UK today.

Birth and fertility rates

The birth rate refers to the number of live births per 1,000 of the population over a year, while the fertility rate refers to the number of live births per 1,000 women aged 15–44 over 1 year. The total fertility rate (TFR) refers to the number of children that are born to an average woman during her childbearing life.

Birth rates in the UK have been in decline for some time. For example, in 1901 there were over a million births but in 2013 only 698,512 babies were born. Fertility rates

Exam tip

Do not worry about learning specific statistics but do attempt to learn trends, that is, know whether something is rising or falling and whether that rise or fall is slight or dramatic.

for England and Wales too have generally declined over the past 100 years: in 1900 the fertility rate was 115, compared with only 57 in 1999, although it had recovered to 64 by 2010. Hicks and Allen (1999) note that in 1900 the total fertility rate was equivalent to a completed family size of 3.5 children. In 2012, the UK's TFR was only 1.94. The consequence of this fall in fertility rates is that families today are significantly smaller compared with the past.

Exam tip

If you are asked to identify two trends relating to birth or fertility rates, make sure these are sufficiently different from each other.

There are a number of reasons for the decline in both the birth rate and the fertility rate in the past 50 years. First, during the twentieth century, childhood became commercialised, which meant that having babies and raising children became an expensive business. For example, it was estimated in 2014 that parents spent 28% of their income on their offspring. Parents today, therefore, may choose to have fewer children for financial reasons.

Second, there is some evidence that women's attitudes to childbearing underwent significant change in the later part of the twentieth century because of the **feminisation of the economy and workforce**. Women today may no longer see childbearing as a priority compared with their mothers and grandmothers. Young women may be more career orientated and more willing to postpone marriage, childbearing and family life. Third, the easy availability of contraception especially the pill on the NHS now gives women control over when to have children and how many to have.

Statistical evidence supports the validity of this argument in three ways. First, the average age of married women giving birth has increased by 6 years since 1971 to nearly 30 in 2012. Second, fertility rates for women aged between 35 and 39 have doubled in the past 40 years, while those for women aged below 30 have declined. Moreover, the number of children born to women aged 40 and over has more than doubled in the last 30 years. Third, society has seen the emergence of a relatively new lifestyle choice among women — **voluntary childlessness**. The Family Policy Studies Centre found that, in 2000, one in five women aged 40, many of them graduates, had deliberately chosen not to have children, compared with one in ten in 1980.

The ageing of the population

The period 1983–2013 saw a 13% fall in the UK death rate. Only 576,000 deaths occurred in Britain in 2013 despite a population of approximately 64 million. Moreover, life expectancy in the UK has also increased. Male children born in 2013 will, on average, live for 78.7 years while females will, on average, live for 82.6 years. Around one in three babies born in 2013 will live to be 100 years old.

These positive trends are the result of a number of factors, including improved nutrition, better standards of living and improvements in housing, the welfare state (especially the provision of pensions) and the NHS (especially mass vaccination and advances in drug technology and surgery), which now mean that more people than ever are likely to survive bouts of cancer, heart disease and other life-threatening

Feminisation of the economy and workforce
From the 1970s, the British economy underwent significant change and the jobs traditionally dominated by men went into decline. However, the female-dominated service economy started to grow, which resulted in large numbers of women going out to work.

Voluntary childlessness
There is an increasing trend for career women to deliberately choose not to have children for a variety of reasons. Some sociologists dislike the term 'childless' because it implies that those who do not have children would like to have them. They prefer the term 'childfree'.

Knowledge check 25

Identify four reasons why both the birth rate and the fertility rate have declined in the last 50 years.

diseases and to live longer even if they have these diseases. Furthermore, numerous NHS preventative health campaigns have raised awareness of health-threatening behaviour and persuaded people to change their lifestyles with regard to smoking, drinking, diet and exercise, for example.

As a result of increased life expectancy and the decline in the birth and fertility rates, the UK is experiencing an ageing of the population. In the UK today, there are increasing numbers of people aged 65 and over and declining numbers of children under 16.

Family diversity

Functionalist and New Right sociologists celebrate the nuclear family unit. Most families, as Chester points out, are nuclear in structure but there are signs in the UK of growing family diversity. As a result of divorce, falling birth and fertility rates, the ageing of the population, global migration and changing attitudes, especially among women, there is evidence that the number of alternative family and household types is increasing. Postmodernists such as Stacey argue that family life in the UK today is pluralistic, that is, family life is now diverse.

Structural diversity

This refers to diversity in terms of family size. Divorce, decline in the birth, fertility and death rates and changing attitudes of women have been responsible for the increased importance of one-parent families, reconstituted families, extended families and beanpole families as well as the increased number of single-person households.

One-parent families

In 2012, the ONS estimated that there were approximately 2 million single-parent families in Britain, making up about a quarter of all families. In the same year, 91% of single-parent families were headed by women. Of these single mothers, 49% were separated, divorced or widowed but a fast-growing group since 2000 have been female single parents who have never married or cohabited. Contrary to popular belief, this group is not composed of teenagers, who in fact make up less than 2% of single parents. Instead, an increasing number of middle-class career women are electing to have children in their late 30s and early 40s and such women are choosing to bring these children up alone. However, New Right sociologists suggest that there is also a large group of single mothers who have never married or cohabited, who are long-term unemployed and less educated, and who are attracted to lone motherhood by the 'perverse incentive' of being able to claim welfare benefits.

New Right sociologists typically see the latter type of lone-parent family as an inherently second-rate and 'broken' family type. They argue that children from such families lack self-discipline and are often emotionally disturbed because of the lack of a firm father figure in their lives. They claim that such children are likely to be members of a criminal and welfare-dependent underclass who are likely to underachieve at school and are the main cause of social problems such as drug abuse, juvenile delinquency and antisocial behaviour.

However, in defence of one-parent families, feminist sociologists such as Phoenix maintain that the single-parent family is unfairly discriminated against because of familial ideology which emphasises the nuclear family ideal. This ideal leads to the negative labelling of

Pluralistic This means that family life in the UK is now characterised by choice, diversity, variation and instability rather than by sameness.

Exam tip

Make sure that you are able to explain the origins of different types of family.

one-parent families by teachers, social workers, housing departments, the police and the courts. Moreover, studies by Ford and Millar argue that the 'perverse incentive' argument is fundamentally flawed when the quality of life of lone parents is examined. Many experience poverty, debt and material hardship despite being paid state benefits. Ford and Millar suggest poverty is the major cause of single parenthood. Single women from poor socioeconomic backgrounds living on council estates with higher than average rates of unemployment are more likely than others to become solo mothers. Motherhood is regarded as a desired and valued goal by these women because it is a realistic alternative to their poor economic prospects. Finally, Mooney et al. suggests that parental conflict is more important than parental separation as an influence in producing negative outcomes in children. Being brought up by a single parent may be more beneficial than being in a family in which the parents are constantly fighting.

Single parenthood is rarely a permanent state. It lasts about 5 years on average and most single parents remarry and form another type of nuclear family in which a father is present — the stepfamily. Also, it is rarely reported that the majority of one-parent families bring up their children successfully to be relatively well-adjusted and law-abiding citizens and workers.

The reconstituted family

Stepfamilies or reconstituted families are one of the fastest-growing types of family in the UK. The main causes of this family form are divorce and remarriage. For example, in 2009, 19.1% of marriages involved the remarriage of one partner, while 15.8% involved the remarriage of both partners. In 2013, the ONS estimated that 8% of families, about 540,000 in all, in England and Wales were stepfamilies and that one in three people in the UK are now a step-parent, stepchild, adult stepchild, stepsibling or step-grandparent. Most (78%) consisted of a natural mother, her offspring and a stepfather.

Reconstituted families are unique because children are also likely to have close ties with their other natural parent. An increasing number of children experience co-parenting, where they spend half their week with their mother and stepfather and spend the other half with their father. Some family experts see co-parenting as a characteristic of bi-nuclear families — two separate post-divorce or post-separation households are really one family system as far as children are concerned.

De'Ath and Slater's study of step-parenting identified a number of challenges facing reconstituted families. For example, children may find themselves pulled in two directions, especially if the relationship between their natural parents continues to be strained, conflict may be a norm if the stepchild refuses to accept the authority of the step-parent, and the birth of a half-sibling may create jealousy and resentment among the stepchildren.

Knowledge check 27

What is a bi-nuclear family?

Extended families

It was generally thought until fairly recently that the extended family that resided under the same roof was in terminal decline. Wall found that in the 1950s 40% of elderly people lived with their relatives but this had dropped to only 5% by the mid-1990s. However, there are signs that the extended family in which adult children are caring for an aged parent in either the same or an attached residence may be experiencing a revival. Victor estimated that 10% of 65-plus-year-olds now live in this type of family.

However, extended kinship ties do not necessarily mean sharing a residence. Extended kin may live nearby and see and support each other on a regular basis. Research by Hoban et al. found that 78% of their elderly sample saw their adult children at least once a week. Chambers noted that an increasing number of elderly people are using communication technologies such as telephone, e-mail, Skyping and Facebook to keep in contact with their extended kin.

However, feminist sociologists have suggested that care of elderly relatives in extended families is likely to impact negatively on the lives of daughters rather than sons because females tend to take on a disproportionate responsibility for the care of elderly parents compared with men. Such caring responsibilities mean that women cannot participate in the full-time labour market and therefore become economically dependent on their husbands. There is also evidence that caring for elderly relatives can create financial hardship, and even poverty, for families, especially if one of the spouses has to give up work.

Beanpole families

Brannen argues that the ageing of the population and the decline in fertility have led to the recent emergence of **beanpole families**.

Brannen argues that families are now more likely to experience vertical intergenerational ties, that is, closer ties with grandparents and great-grandparents. She argues that the 'pivot generation' (that is, grandparents) who are sandwiched between older and younger family generations is increasingly in demand to provide for the needs of both their elderly parents and their grandchildren. For example, 20% of people in their fifties and sixties currently care for a parent, while 10% care for both a parent and a grandchild. Such services are based on the assumption of 'reciprocity', that is, the provision of babysitting services for grandchildren, for example, might be balanced by the assumption that the grandchildren's parents will assist their parents in their old age.

Elderly-couple households

An ageing population means that the number of elderly couples living independently in their own household as either married or cohabiting spouses is increasing — from 52.6% of the elderly population in 2001 to 56.8% in 2011. Elderly couples are likely to remain in their own home. Only 3.7% of elderly people lived in sheltered housing or residential homes in 2011 and the majority of those in the latter type of institution were aged over 85.

Single-person households

The ageing of the population has led to a significant increase in the number of one-person households over state pension age as a proportion of all households. In 2013, 14% of all households and nearly half of all one-person households were of this type, a total of 3.6 million households. Of those aged 65 and over who live alone, 68% are female because, on average, women live longer than men and they tend to marry men older than themselves. In 2013, there were 1.7 million widowed women aged 65 or over living alone in the UK. This was three times the number of widowers. Chambers refers to this trend as the 'feminisation of later life'.

Beanpole families
These are four-generational families — families that include great-grandparents and great-grandchildren but have few aunts, uncles and cousins. Consequently, children today have fewer siblings compared with previous generations of children.

Knowledge check 28

Why have beanpole families become more common?

In 2013, about 16% of all households, that is 4.1 million people, were composed of people aged *under* 65 years. A number of trends can be perceived with regard to those groups most likely to live in this type of household.

- The majority of these single households —58% — were male because males are more likely than females to never marry.
- The number of middle-aged single people living alone has increased because of divorce.
- Young professional women are marrying later and in the meantime are choosing to live alone.
- The number of young working-class people choosing to live alone has fallen by about a fifth in the last 20 years because of youth unemployment and the fact that they can no longer afford to enter the rented housing market.

Living apart but together (LATs)

One in ten people in Britain today has made what is seen as a growing, and increasingly acceptable, lifestyle choice known as LAT ('living apart together'), in which couples who regard themselves as firmly committed to each other have separate homes through choice or circumstance. Duncan et al. found that LATs are predominantly young. They found that LATs chose to live apart because they desired a certain amount of freedom and independence or because constraints such as money or unsuitable accommodation made living together difficult.

Cultural diversity

Cultural diversity refers to the impact of global migration on family structures and dynamics. Mass migration into Britain of Asian and African-Caribbean people in the 1950s and 1960s has had a significant cultural effect on family life in the UK. The evidence suggests that there may be important differences in the way Asians and African-Caribbeans organise their family life.

Berthoud's research found that about a third of Asian families in the UK live in extended families because Asian children feel a strong sense of duty and obligation towards their parents. Moreover, Asian people also feel a strong sense of duty to assist economically extended kin who may live in other countries. Berthoud also found that Asians were more likely to marry younger than white people and that they were more likely to disapprove of cohabitation and divorce. Marriage in Asian families — whether Muslim, Hindu or Sikh — is still mainly arranged (that is, negotiated with children rather than forced) and there is little intermarriage with other religions or cultures.

African-Caribbean communities have a higher proportion of one-parent families compared with white communities — over 50% of African-Caribbean families with children are one-parent families. The main reason for the high number of single-parent families according to Chamberlain is the increasing trend of African-Caribbean mothers choosing to live independently from their children's father. Two-thirds of 20-year-old African-Caribbean mothers remain single compared with only 11% of their white peers.

Berthoud suggests that the attitudes of young African-Caribbean women are characterised by modern individualism — they are choosing to bring up children alone in matrifocal families for two reasons. First, it is probable that African-Caribbean

Knowledge check 29

Identify four different groups that make up the single-person household population in the UK.

Exam tip

The material on ethnic identity can be used to supplement this material.

women rationally weigh up the costs and benefits of living with the fathers of their children and conclude that African-Caribbean men are unreliable as a source of family income and potentially a financial burden because they are likely to be unemployed. Second, Chamberlain and Goulbourne found that African-Caribbean single mothers are often supported by an extended kinship network which includes both blood relatives and fictive kin.

Dual-heritage or mixed-race families

Platt indicates that African-Caribbeans are more likely than any other ethnic minority group to intermarry with members of another ethnic group, especially white people. The number of mixed-race partnerships means that only a minority of African-Caribbean men and women are married to fellow African-Caribbeans and only one-quarter of African-Caribbean children live with two black parents.

Ali notes that such marriages result in interethnic families and mixed-race (sometimes called 'dual-heritage') children. Platt found that the number of mixed-race children has grown considerably in recent years. For example, since the turn of the twenty-first century the number of children of Caribbean heritage with one white parent has risen from 39% to 49%. Young people aged 18 and under are six times more likely to be mixed race than people aged 30 plus. Some sociologists have suggested that these types of families have their own unique problems, such as facing prejudice and discrimination from both white and black communities.

Sexual diversity

In 1999, the law lords ruled that a homosexual couple can be legally defined as a family. In 2014, gay marriage was legalised, which means that long-term same-sex partners have similar rights to heterosexual married couples with regard to inheritance (of property and pensions, for example) and next-of-kin status. It is estimated that there are 6,000 gay couples living together in the UK and there were approximate 1,400 gay marriages between March and June of 2014.

There has also been an increase in same-sex families because the Adoption and Children Act (2002) gave same-sex couples the right to adopt children, while the Human Fertilisation and Embryology Act (2009) legally recognised lesbians and their partners as parents in cases of in-vitro fertilisation or assisted/self-insemination.

Class diversity

This refers to social-class variations in the quality of family relationships and lifestyles. For example, upper-class family life may be very different to that experienced by middle-class or working-class families. Some sociologists argue that middle-class parents are more child-centred than working-class parents. They supposedly take a greater interest in their children's education, and consequently pass on economic, social and cultural advantages which assist their children through the educational system. However, critical sociologists argue that working-class parents are just as child-centred, but that material deprivation or poverty limits how much help they can give their children. Therefore, the working-class child's experience is likely to be less satisfactory because of family poverty, poor schools, lack of material support, greater risks of accidents both in the home and in the street, and so on.

Fictive kin People who are unrelated, such as family friends and neighbours, who have an emotional attachment to the family and are consequently treated as aunts and uncles.

Knowledge check 30

Identify two potential problems faced by mixed-race children.

Postmodernism

Postmodernists such as Stacey argue that in the postmodern era, families are very varied in the structure and form that they take because they are constantly changing and have no set structure that can be regarded as an ideal. They argue that, as a result of this, sociological studies of the family should focus on the 'life courses' of individuals rather than 'the family'.

In other words, sociologists should examine the way lives evolve and change as people experience rites of passage such as marriage, the birth of a child or the death of a partner and significant life events such as divorce, remarriage, step-relationships, cohabitation, dual-parenting, family feuds or children leaving home. Life-course analysis, therefore, focuses on the diversity of family practices that occur during the life course.

Stacey argues that families and households are not static concrete things because family life is in a continual state of flux and change. There is therefore no such thing as the perfect family because interactions between family members and the family dynamics that result are unique to that group of people. If every experience of family is different there can be no universal criteria by which 'families' can be judged as right or wrong.

Pahl and Spencer argue that the concept of 'family' is becoming obsolete because of the growing importance of 'non-family households'. They believe that people no longer feel they have to maintain relationships with family members out of a sense of duty or obligation. Instead people are now more likely to subscribe to 'personal communities' made up of a combination of relatives, fictive kin and friends who are valued for their friendship and social support. They therefore argue that friendship networks and households (for example, sharing a flat or house with friends or fellow students) often now function as if they were families. Roseneil also argues such friendships are no longer tied together by heterosexuality. In 2015, it is common for heterosexuals to have strong intimate relationships with gay people.

Finally, Smart argues that the concept of 'personal life' is more neutral and flexible than the concept of 'family' because it goes beyond marriage and biological kin to include newer types of relationships such as post-divorce relationships, same-sex relationships, relationships created by new reproductive technologies, relationships in which people commit to each other but live apart, open relationships and friendships.

'Life course' Hareven (2000) notes that the life course is made up of several stages: birth, early childhood, infancy, childhood, adolescence, young adulthood, adulthood, middle age and old age.

Exam tip

Most of this postmodernist material is highly evaluative and therefore well worth learning.

Non-family households Households that contain people who may not be related to one another but who choose to live and socialise together as friends. It is suggested that friendships are now just as important as family relationships.

Summary

- Functionalist and New Right sociologists believe that the nuclear family is beneficial for both society and the individual.
- Marxists and feminists are generally critical of the way family life is organised.
- New Right sociologists believe that the nuclear family is under threat because of the decline of marriage, the increasing popularity of cohabitation, divorce and the rise in the number of one-parent families.
- The decline in the birth, fertility and death rates has led to increasing diversity in family types and lifestyles.
- Diversity exists in family life but also in personal relationships and non-family households.

To what extent are roles and relationships within families and households changing?

Roles and relationships between partners: the domestic division of labour

In their study of working-class families in the East End of London in the 1950s, Young and Wilmott had observed that **conjugal roles** and the **domestic division of labour** in working-class families were clearly segregated. Men were primarily wage earners and were responsible for very few domestic tasks around the home while most women were full-time housewives. However, Young and Wilmott claimed that the 1970s saw the growing popularity of a new type of nuclear family — the symmetrical family, which was underpinned by egalitarian marriage in which all domestic roles were jointly shared.

Feminists such as Oakley have rejected the notion of a symmetrical family. She argued that patriarchy was still very much a major characteristic of modern nuclear families and that women still occupied a subordinate and dependent role within the family and in wider society. This feminist critique is supported by the fact that there is little hard evidence in the twenty-first century for equality in marriage. Research by Craig in 2007 found that women do between one-third and one-half more housework than men. She argues that this inequality begins when a couple move in together and before they have children. She calls this aspect of domestic inequality the 'partnership penalty'. Her research found that when couples marry, the wife's unpaid domestic labour rises in volume while the husband does less housework compared with when he was single. A survey of 1,000 men and women by the BBC in 2014 argued that modern marriage was characterised by 'chore wars' rather than equality and symmetry. It found evidence of consistent conflict between partners over domestic chores. Two-thirds of those aged between 18 and 34 years admitted that they regularly argued with their partners over housework. Women were particularly frustrated with their partners over how little they did around the home or about the male standard of cleanliness which many felt did not achieve their standards.

However, there is evidence that the more a woman contributes to the family finances, the more the man does in the home, particularly with regard to childcare. Nevertheless, Craig points out that men only engage with the more enjoyable aspects of childcare whereas women's time with children was spent servicing them. The quantitative evidence regarding the domestic division of labour clearly supports the feminist argument that women today are experiencing a 'second shift' or 'dual burden' with regard to housework. They have two jobs — one paid and one unpaid — and therefore experience the double burden of trying to be effective at both.

The notion that men and women share decision making in families was questioned by research carried out by Hardill et al., who discovered that middle-class wives generally deferred to their husbands in major decisions about where to live, the size of the mortgage or buying cars, for example. They concluded that the men in their sample were able to demand that the interests of their wives and families should be subordinated to the man's career because he was the major breadwinner.

Conjugal roles The roles and responsibilities of spouses — for example, the male may be the breadwinner.

Domestic division of labour How spouses divide up housework and childcare tasks.

Knowledge check 31

Explain what is meant by a symmetrical family.

Knowledge check 32

Explain what is meant by the partnership penalty and chore wars.

Exam tip

Learn the names of these sociologists. Their studies constitute evidence which is rewarded as part of the application and analysis skills.

Duncombe and Marsden argue that any measurement of equality within households must take account of 'emotion work'. They argue that women take the major responsibility for the emotional wellbeing and happiness of their partners and children in addition to paid work and responsibility for housework and childcare. In this sense, women work a **triple shift**. Hochschild argues that mothers are rarely thanked for this work because what they do is gender bound — it is seen by other family members as part of their gendered duty. For example, if the father provides childcare, it is often interpreted by him as a gift to the mother but this is not so if the mother provides it because it is seen as her job.

Explanations for inequalities in the domestic division of labour

Functionalists see the sexual division of labour in the home as brought about primarily by biological differences between the sexes. Parsons, for example, argued that women are 'naturally' suited to the caring of the young because of the fact that they physically bear children, while Murdock cited the greater physical strength of the male as the reason why men were able to dominate economic life.

Feminist sociologists have long blamed familial ideology — the dominant idea that there is an ideal way to organise family life — for inequalities in power in the home. This familial ideology shapes cultural expectations about femininity, which is still primarily associated with motherhood and homemaking despite the feminisation of the economy and workforce. Leonard argues that men resist change because the persistence of an unequal division of labour suits them.

Marxist-feminist analysis claims the inequality in domestic labour persists because it benefits capitalism. They point out that such work is unpaid but that it has great value for capitalist economies. For example, Benston suggests that the nuclear family, and especially women's nurturing role within it, is important to capitalism because it produces and rears the future workforce at little cost to the capitalist state. She also points out that women's unpaid domestic labour — housework as well as sexual services — ensures that the male workforce is fit and healthy to work and consequently productive. The housework role therefore contributes to the effectiveness of male labour and the value of the work he produces for his employer.

Hakim rejects the idea that the distribution of domestic labour is shaped by biology, patriarchal ideology or capitalism. She suggests that some women rationally choose to be mothers and housewives and that such women therefore have less commitment to work compared with men. She argues that women generally feel they have two main choices in life: some choose employment and commit themselves to juggling the dual burden of paid work and domestic responsibilities, while others choose the marriage career. Hakim argues that these women are more than happy to support their husband's careers by taking on the bulk of the domestic work and are not interested in wielding equal power in the home.

Roles and relationships between partners: the dark side of the family

Living in nuclear families can sometimes be dysfunctional or harmful to its members. There is a 'dark side' to family life in that families are the context in which violence most commonly takes place. Most recorded murders, assaults and child abuse, sexual or otherwise, take place within the family unit. There are three

The triple shift The idea that women perform three roles: paid work outside the family, most of the housework and childcare, as well as responsibility for the emotional maintenance of family members.

Knowledge check 33

Identify three major social problems uniquely associated with families.

domestic killings of women each fortnight on average in the UK, accounting for about 40% of all female murders. Three-quarters of all violence is domestic (and these are only the reported cases).

The child-centred family and the extension of childhood

The social historian Aries suggests that what children experience today as childhood is a recent **social invention** or **construction**. Aries claims that in preindustrial society, the type of childhood that exists in modern societies like the UK today simply did not exist. He argues that as soon as children were no longer physically dependent on their parents, that is, around the age of 7 years, they were treated no differently to adults. Childhood did not extend beyond this age. He argues that children in medieval societies were treated as 'miniature adults' who took part in the same work and play activities as grown-ups. Moreover, during the early industrial period, working-class children were frequently found working in factories, mines and mills in which they were often killed or injured and exposed to toxic substances which shortened their lives.

Aries claims that social attitudes towards children started to change radically in the middle of the nineteenth century. Factory Acts were passed, which excluded children from the mines and certain types of mill and factory work, and reduced the number of hours they could do paid work. Mass education for those aged 5–12 was introduced in 1870 and became compulsory in 1880, which meant that school was a common childhood experience by the beginning of the twentieth century.

The twentieth century therefore saw the emergence of a child-centred society in which childhood was seen as a distinct and separate category from adulthood. Cunningham notes that this child-centred society has three major features: first, children are viewed as innocent, vulnerable and dependent beings in need of adult protection from a range of potential 'threats' such as bad parenting, neglect and exploitation; second, children occupy their own spaces such as the home and school and are excluded from adult spaces such as the workplace; and third, childhood is now associated with certain moral and legal rights such as the right to happiness and good health.

The state too has contributed to the social construction of childhood as a sacred and special period in the life cycle. The twentieth century saw a massive increase in state interference in family life, which was justified by the need to protect children and childhood. Wells notes that the government of childhood is almost entirely organised around saving children from internal threats (e.g. neglectful or abusive parents) and external threats (e.g. germs and viruses, media representations of violence, pornography, exploitation by employers). In this sense, the state aims to take responsibility for the emotional, physical, intellectual and spiritual development of children so that they grow up to be normal law-abiding citizens.

Roles and relationships between parents and children

State family policy and the law are central today in defining and shaping parental responsibility towards children. The state sets out the duties of parents and gives them rights over children's bodies and time. However, some critics argue that the state does not always protect children. Some governments seem to be reluctant to legislate with regard to parental violence, that is, the smacking of children. It is banned in

The social construction of childhood The idea that the nature and quality of childhood depends on the society or time-period in which it exists. Aries argues that childhood as we know it today is a recent social invention.

30 countries, including Scotland, but is legal and socially acceptable in England and Wales, the USA, Canada and Australia.

Some New Right sociologists such as Palmer argue that parents are too happy to use television, electronic games and junk food to keep children occupied. Children are therefore deprived of traditional childhood and family life, and consequently, Palmer claims, children have become more distractible, self-centred and antisocial.

Chambers identifies a tension between parents and children caused by children's use of new media and the rise of a youth-centred media and 'screen-rich bedroom culture'. Adolescents now spend significant amounts of leisure time in the privacy of their own bedrooms, using gaming consoles and laptops in a solitary way. Livingstone notes children communicate more with the virtual outside world than with adult members of their own family. Parents often have to text or Facebook their children to gain their attention at mealtimes.

The relationship between grandparents, parents and children

There is evidence that the ageing of the population has led to a growing recognition that families benefit from the presence of grandparents and that the interaction between grandparents and grandchildren is more qualitative compared with the past. Grandparents today are more healthy and active compared with previous generations. Consequently, they make a significant contribution to the parenting and socialisation process.

It is estimated that 5.8 million grandparents currently look after their grandchildren regularly for an average of 10 hours a week, that is, 47% of the nation's grandparents. This amounts to families saving nearly £11bn in childcare costs over a year.

Ross et al. found that grandparents spoke positively about being a grandparent and were happy to help with childcare and to give advice and support to their grandchildren. Many young people said they could share problems and concerns with their grandparents. Grandparents would sometimes act as go-betweens in the family when children fell out with their parents.

> **Exam tip**
>
> Notice the emphasis on social change. You need to have a clear idea of how childhood has changed over time. Be aware that questions may be time specific — for example, they may stress change over the past 200 years or 100 years.

Summary

- The view that there is equality or symmetry in marriage is not supported by either the quantitative or the qualitative research.
- Childhood as we know it today is a relatively recent social invention.
- The experience of childhood is also relative and is dependent on social factors such as social class, ethnicity, religion, gender and region.
- A number of sociologists perceive a decline in childhood as an innocent age as children are increasingly exposed to adult concerns via new media.
- Grandparents are playing an increasingly important role in family life, especially in the socialisation of children.

Questions & Answers

How to use this section

In this section you will find three questions at AS and three at A-level. The question numbering for both the AS and A-level questions is the same as you will find in the examination. While the structure and mark allocation of AS and A-level are different, there is no harm in reading through and trying the 'other' questions — indeed, it will serve as good revision.

Each question part is followed by a brief analysis of what to watch out for when answering it (shown by the icon **e**). Each then has an A-grade answer, with commentary throughout (preceded by the icon **e**), indicating where credit is due.

Read each question carefully, and either try to answer it in full or at least make notes of how you would answer it *before* reading the student answer and comments. This might help to pick up on mistakes you have made or things that you are doing well.

As a general point, you should always read through the whole question before starting to write. When you come to answer the question that is based on a source, read it carefully, as it will contain material that is essential to answering the question.

Remember that there is no single perfect way of answering an exam question — the highest marks can be gained by taking different approaches, especially in the higher-mark questions. However, the comments should help to show you the kinds of approach that would do well, and some of the pitfalls to avoid. In particular, the comments tell you what it is that enables the student to score so highly. Attention is given to the student's use of the examinable skills: knowledge and understanding, application, and analysis and evaluation.

Examinable skills

OCR sociology examination papers are designed to test certain defined skills. These skills are expressed as assessment objectives (AOs) and are the same for AS and A-level, though the weighting given to each differs between the two levels. There are three AOs and it is important that you know what these are and what you have to be able to do in an exam to show your ability in each. Further guidance on each of the AOs is given below and in the comments. In practice, the A-grade answers, particularly those carrying the higher marks, will contain elements of all three AOs.

Assessment objective 1 (AO1)

Demonstrate knowledge and understanding of:
- **sociological theories, concepts and evidence**
- **sociological research methods**

Your exam answers will have to demonstrate clearly to the examiners that your knowledge is accurate and appropriate to the topic being discussed and that you have a clear understanding of it. It is not enough simply to reproduce knowledge learned by rote. You must be able to use your knowledge of concepts, sociological studies, evidence and sociological theories in a meaningful and logical way to answer and illustrate with examples the specific question set.

Assessment objective 2 (AO2)

Apply sociological theories, concepts, evidence and research methods to a range of issues.

This means that you must be able to demonstrate the ability to address the question throughout your response by consistently applying relevant sociological concepts, studies and theories.

Some of the questions specifically focused on socialisation, culture and identity in the exam will instruct you to use the source(s) that precedes the question — this may be a photograph, graph or piece of text, for example, which sets the context for the question that is to follow, and which provides you with some information to help answer it. You *must* take this relevant information and use (apply) it in your answer. However, 'applying' the material does not mean simply copying it from the source and leaving it to speak for itself. You will need to show your understanding of the material by doing something with it, such as offering a criticism, explaining something about it, linking it to a particular sociological theory or using it as an example of what is being stated or suggested. You will also be expected to use your own knowledge to add to the information that you have been given and to apply it appropriately to answer the question.

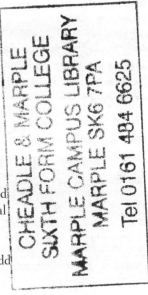

Assessment objective 3 (AO3)

Analyse and evaluate sociological theories, concepts, evidence and research methods in order to:

- **present arguments**
- **make judgements**
- **draw conclusions**

The skill of *analysis* is shown by breaking something down into its component parts and subjecting them to detailed examination. Analysis is therefore shown by providing answers (depending, of course, on what it is that you are analysing) to questions which instruct you to explain, and to assess or evaluate specific sociological views or theories. It involves asking questions such as 'who said or who believes this?', 'what does this concept relate to?', 'how was this evidence collected?' and so on. The skill of *evaluation* is shown by the ability to identify the strengths and weaknesses or limitations of any sociological material. It is not sufficient, however, simply to list the strengths or limitations of something — you need to be able to say *why* something is considered a strength or otherwise, and sometimes you will need to state *who* claims that this is a strength or weakness. Depending on what it is you are discussing, you may be able to reach a credible and supported conclusion about the relative merits or otherwise of something. This means that it should be based on the sociological arguments and evidence that you have presented during your answer.

Weighting of assessment objectives

In the exam papers, each AO is given a particular weighting, which indicates its relative importance to the overall mark gained. The weightings are not the same for AS and A-level, so be sure that you look at the one that is appropriate for the exam you will be taking.

Table 1 Weighting for AS examinations

Component	% of OCR AS in Sociology (H180)		
	AO1	AO2	AO3
Socialisation, culture and identity (H180/01)	45–50%	30–35%	15–20%
Researching and understanding social inequalities (H180/02)	45–50%	25–30%	20–25%

Table 2 Weighting for A-level examinations

Component	% of OCR A-level in Sociology (H580)		
	AO1	AO2	AO3
Socialisation, culture and identity (H580/01)	40–45%	40–45%	15–20%
Researching and understanding social inequalities (H580/02)	30–35%	30–35%	35–40%
Debates in contemporary society (H580/03)	40–45%	20–25%	30–35%

Command words

Ofqual, the body that sets the criteria for all GCE sociology specifications, has an approved list of 'command words' that are used in exam questions. The following are some of the most commonly used, but it is important to remember that the list is not exhaustive, and that occasionally other, similar, words or phrases may be used instead. This shows how important it is to take time in an exam and read the questions carefully before you start writing. It is worth learning what is meant by these command words, to ensure that you give an appropriate response.

Define Give the meaning of something.

Explain Describe the purposes of something or give reasons for it.

Describe/Outline Give the main characteristics of a concept or sociological view.

Outline and explain Give the main characteristics of a sociological view and develop these by referencing studies and using examples.

Using the source and your wider sociological knowledge, explain Draw on the material provided and develop it using your own knowledge to answer the question.

Identify and briefly explain Recognise and give examples of something and explain its purpose or reasons for its existence.

Evaluate/Assess Make judgements from the available evidence.

■ The AS examination

The topics of socialisation, culture and identity and the option 'Families and relationships' are examined on Paper 1 of the AS examination, **Socialisation, culture and identity**. The questions on socialisation, culture and identity appear in Section A of Paper 1 as questions 1–4. These are a mixture of short and medium compulsory questions. Some are based on source material. Section A questions add up to 30 marks altogether, or 40% of the paper.

The four questions on families and relationships appear in Section B, Option 1 as questions 5–8. These are a mixture of short, medium and extended compulsory questions. Section B questions add up to 45 marks altogether, or 60% of the paper.

The whole exam lasts for 1 hour 30 minutes, carries 75 marks and is worth 50% of the AS qualification. It is worth spending about 35 minutes on Section A and 55 minutes on Section B. Try to manage your time so that you have enough spare to read through your responses to the whole paper at the end.

AS question 1

Socialisation, culture and identity

Read the source material and answer questions 1–4.

British culture is made up of people agreeing to share beliefs, values, norms, traditions and so on. However, in a multicultural society like the UK, there also exist social groups who subscribe to values and norms which may differ from the mainstream. These groups generally conform to British culture but practise distinct cultural ways based on religion, ethnicity and even social class.

1   Define the concept of 'subculture'.   (4 marks)

ⓔ Always use an example to illustrate your definition in order to demonstrate your understanding.

2   With reference to the source, identify and briefly explain two examples of subculture.   (6 marks)

ⓔ You must make clear reference to both the photograph and the text.

3   Using the source and your wider sociological knowledge, explain how values are relative.   (8 marks)

ⓔ This is asking for two detailed paragraphs. Use lots of examples to display your understanding.

4   Explain and briefly evaluate the view that the dominant values and norms associated with femininity today are very different from those held by previous generations.   (12 marks)

ⓔ Start by discussing the hegemonic definitions held by previous generations. Show how males and females were socialised into these by the family, education and so on. The latter half of the essay should identify how and why masculinity and femininity are changing (although you should question the degree of change compared with the past).

Families and relationships

5   Define and briefly explain the idea of 'expressive' and 'instrumental roles'.   (5 marks)

ⓔ Make sure you identify the source of these concepts and that when you define them you use examples of specific tasks to illustrate them.

6   Identify and briefly describe two changes in childhood that have occurred over the last 100 years.   (8 marks)

ⓔ Try to choose two very different changes to avoid overlap. Think about the time frame — obviously all change before 1915 is off-limits.

7   Explain reasons for the rise in the divorce rate since 1972.   (12 marks)

ⓔ At least five reasons could be referred to in reasonable detail — note the deliberate reference to 1972. References to pre-1972 will not be rewarded.

8   Evaluate the view that the domestic division of labour in many marriages is now equal.   (20 marks)

ⓔ Do not make the mistake of thinking you have to agree with the question. However, you do have to outline the pro-equality arguments. Evaluate using a wide selection of feminist studies including Craig and concepts such as the double and triple shift.

Student answer

1 A subculture is a social group that is generally happy to abide by the general culture of a society. For example, it will obey the laws of society and agree with many of its values. However, subcultures based on ethnicity may have their own very distinct culture and religion which they wish to keep alive through use of language, dress and diet and unique forms of religious worship.

ⓔ This response is both precise and comprehensive. It highlights the fact that most subcultures are happy to exist both within and alongside mainstream culture. It focuses on ethnicity, which is a valid thing to do, and intelligently identifies four aspects of subcultural identity. This response demonstrates excellent knowledge and understanding and is awarded full marks. **4/4 marks awarded.**

2 The source refers to religious subcultures. Sikhs are a very distinct religious subculture in the UK — they have built temples in British cities, they celebrate religious festivals, the men wear turbans as a symbol of their Sikh identity and family members may speak Punjabi at home.

The photograph in Source A identifies a member of a spectacular youth subculture called punks. Many of these subcultures were seen as deviant by mainstream society because they dressed in styles that shocked society and behaved in ways that caused public concern.

ⓔ The student is awarded the full 2 marks for knowledge and understanding because they have successfully identified two subcultures and the full 4 marks for application because of the focus on the source and because the illustration addresses the question throughout. **6/6 marks awarded.**

3 The source refers to ethnic minorities who often have values which may be different to those held by the majority population. There is some evidence that people from Asian subcultures living in the UK may have different cultural values to white people. For example, Asian people value marriage like white people do. However, young people are more likely to marry someone they hardly know because their parents (with their permission) have arranged the marriage with the family of the bride or bridegroom. As a result, they do not expect to be in love when they marry but their culture expects them to work hard at marriage and to eventually fall in love. Divorce is very low as a result. In contrast, white people expect to marry because they are in love.

The source also refers to subcultures that are based on social class. It can be argued that people from middle-class and working-class backgrounds belong to separate subcultures because they often believe in different values.

> For example, some sociologists believe middle-class people are more likely to value education and, as a result, they are more likely to defer gratification or make sacrifices while working towards some goal like qualifications. They are also more likely to make sure their children have cultural capital — this means they make sure they have the right skills to do well in school. In contrast, sociologists argue that working-class people believe in immediate gratification — if, for example, they come into money, they will spend it straightaway rather than save it.

ⓔ This student demonstrates an excellent ability in terms of knowledge and understanding of how values are relative. Relevant values — cultural values and education — are chosen and are explicitly and accurately applied to the source material. The student consequently scores the full marks for each skill. **8/8 marks awarded.**

4   In the past, expectations about feminine behaviour were very clear. For example, married females were stereotyped according to Tunstall as best suited to the roles of homemaker, wife, romantic, shopper–consumer, mother and emotional caretaker. Wolf also argues that single available women were stereotyped as sexual beings by the media. Their bodies were sexually objectified by features such as Page 3 in the *Sun* newspaper.

ⓔ This paragraph focuses on traditional stereotypes of females . It displays an intelligent grasp of concepts and uses examples and studies in an applied and convincing fashion.

> Many sociologists have argued that these stereotypes are now under attack because of the economic and cultural changes that have occurred over the last few decades. Traditional manual jobs dominated by males have gone into decline, resulting in high rates of male unemployment, while many of the new jobs created in areas like retail and finance have gone to women. Women therefore now have the opportunity to embark on careers in which they earn incomes similar to those of males.

ⓔ The student provides a credible sociological explanation for why traditional stereotypes about femininity are under attack.

> It is claimed that these economic trends have led to cultural changes. For example, Sharpe found that when she repeated her classic research of working-class girls, 'Just Like a Girl', in the mid-1990s, girls no longer saw marriage and children as a priority. In the 1970s similar girls just wanted to get married and start families.
>
> Sociologists have argued that the feminisation of the labour force means men have taken on more emotional caring roles, especially in regard to

childcare. There is no doubt that men are more involved, e.g. more men than ever attend the birth of their children. However, it is probably an exaggeration to talk about a 'new man' in touch with his feminine side. Also, women who work outside the home still do most of the childcare and housework. For example, Craig found that when men and women move in together, she ends up increasing the amount of time she spends on housework but his amount of time goes down. These studies do not show new types of femininity or masculinity.

e The use of Sharpe and Craig clearly illustrates cultural change and the reference to men's roles, while generalised, is focused on evaluation in its questioning of the notion that new masculinities and femininities are appearing.

In conclusion, there is no doubt that femininity today is very different from that of previous generations. Girls today are more likely to value education, go to university and have a career. They also get married and have children later. Some even choose not to have children because it might disrupt their career. However, most men and women eventually settle down in traditional relationships in which traditional ideas about masculinity and femininity are still widely held by both women and men. There is also little evidence that the attitudes and practices of men with regard to paid work and family roles have changed dramatically.

e The student provides an evaluative conclusion that demonstrates a perceptive grasp of the key points and focuses clearly on the issues embodied in the question.

e This response is a good example of the types of skill required for success at AS. It displays an excellent knowledge and understanding of the debate, very good use of evidence and studies as illustration and consequently is awarded the full 4 marks for this skill. Material is well selected and organised, addresses the question throughout and is therefore awarded the full 4 marks for application. Finally, the student displays an excellent ability to analyse and evaluate throughout and is awarded the full 4 marks for this skill. **12/12 marks awarded.**

e Total score for Section A: 30/30 marks. Overall, this is a first-class sociological response to the socialisation, culture and identity questions. The student demonstrates strong knowledge and understanding skills throughout, especially with regard to studies, always addresses the questions and generally analyses and evaluates ideas in a consistent fashion.

5 This is an idea invented by the functionalist sociologist Parsons and refers to the equal but different roles played by husbands and wives in families. Parsons believed that the role of women in families was just as important as that of the man. Parsons saw the male as the instrumental leader who is responsible for the economic welfare of the family as the breadwinner. The female is the expressive leader who takes responsibility for the nurturing of children and the emotional maintenance of the family.

e This is a clear and detailed definition which is theoretically grounded and which explicitly and accurately illustrates the concepts. **5/5 marks awarded.**

> **6** First, the government plays a greater role compared with a century ago in making sure that children have a happy childhood by monitoring the quality of parenting using health visitors and social workers as well as passing laws which protect children against neglect and abuse. The state also takes responsibility for the education of children up to the age of 18. The state also helps children financially by paying child benefit to the mothers of children.
>
> Second, businesses have developed which specialise in childhood products such as prams, clothing and toys. Parents and children are subjected to more advertising today and have access to a greater market of commodities aimed at improving the quality of childhood. There are also media products such as television programmes, magazines and computer games aimed specifically at children.

e Excellent knowledge and understanding is demonstrated and the two changes are explicitly explained and illustrated. **8/8 marks awarded.**

> **7** In 1970, only 60,000 divorces were granted in the UK but by 1993, the number of divorces had trebled to an all-time high. However, the number of divorces in 2012 had fallen to 118,000. If present trends continue, about 40% of current marriages will end in divorce. There are four sociological explanations for this increase in divorce.
>
> First, changes in divorce law, especially the introduction of the Divorce Reform Act in 1970, have generally made it easier and cheaper to end marriages. Before this legislation, divorce was expensive and complex. It involved going to court and 'proving' that the spouse was guilty of a matrimonial 'crime' such as adultery. However, the Divorce Reform Act stated that only a 2-year separation if both agreed was required for a divorce to be granted on the grounds of irretrievable breakdown of marriage. The passing of this Act led to a massive increase in divorce in the 1970s as those trapped in empty-shell marriages took advantage of this new law.
>
> Second, functionalist sociologists argue that social expectations about marriage have changed. They argue that high divorce rates may be evidence that marriage is increasingly valued and that people are demanding higher standards from their partners. Couples are no longer prepared to put up with unhappy, 'empty-shell' marriages.

Third, feminist sociologists like Thorne and Collard note that women's expectations of marriage have radically changed, compared with previous generations. They argue that women expect far more from marriage than men. If husbands fail to live up to their expectations, women may feel the need to look elsewhere.

Finally, postmodernists such as Beck and Beck-Gernsheim argue that society has become more individualistic and selfish. People who are essentially selfish have problems coping with the selflessness demanded by marriage. There may therefore be conflict because spouses might want different things. For example, the wife who has a career may be put under pressure from her husband to have a baby. Resentment and divorce may follow. In postmodern society, people now have more choice in how to live their life. As a result, divorce is now seen as just another lifestyle choice.

However, we must be careful not to exaggerate divorce. Four out of ten marriages may end in divorce but six out of ten succeed; over 75% of children are living with both natural parents who are legally married. These figures suggest that society still places a high value on marriage and the family.

e The student demonstrates a wide range and excellent knowledge and understanding of the reasons for the increase in divorce which are accurately illustrated with a range of theories and sociological evidence. There is a well-developed argument which is both explicitly focused on divorce and highly relevant. **12/12 marks awarded.**

8   Sociologists such as Young and Wilmott argue that changing attitudes to gender roles and increased participation by women in the labour market have led to more equality in modern family life. The functionalist sociologist Parsons too argued that men and women performed separate roles within the family and these were 'equal but different'. Wilmott and Young invented the concept of the symmetrical nuclear family. They claimed that the conjugal relationship between husband and wife in this type of family was becoming more joint, meaning that wives were now going out to work and men were more likely to share childcare, housework and decision making with their wives. This trend towards egalitarian marriage, Wilmott and Young claimed, was caused by the decline in the extended family in which conjugal roles are very traditional and patriarchal as well as the increasing career opportunities in paid employment for women.

e This opening paragraph is clearly focused on the view in the question. Theory, studies and concepts are accurately identified and explained.

However, feminist sociologists strongly oppose the idea that modern marriages are characterised by equality. Oakley's study of housewives in the 1970s found that only a small percentage of husbands shared housework and although more shared in housework it was only with its more enjoyable aspects such as playing with children. More modern data suggest little has changed. For example, research by Craig (2007) found that women do between one-third and one-half more housework than men, while a survey of 1,000 men and women by the BBC in 2014 argued that modern marriage was characterised by 'chore wars' rather than equality and symmetry. It found evidence of consistent conflict between partners over domestic chores.

e This evaluation of the pro-equality position is done well and successfully applies three sociological studies to the argument.

Feminists also argue that women's lives are often characterised by a double burden because they often work full time and still do most of the housework and childcare. Ferri and Smith surveyed fathers and mothers who both worked full time and found that fathers took the main responsibility for childcare in fewer than 4% of all families. Also, Ramos found in 2003 that unemployed men's housework only just matched that of their working wives. There are other inequalities in power and control in modern families. Duncombe and Marsden argue that women experience a triple shift of labour within families — they work full time, they are mainly responsible for housework and childcare and they emotionally maintain and support other family members. Bernard argues that these pressures mean that marriage often makes women literally sick in that they experience more anxiety and depression than men.

e The evaluation of the pro-equality argument continues to develop both logically and perceptively. Studies are used intelligently to assess the validity of the equality argument.

Some sociologists argue that it is not enough just to count household chores. These sociologists have instead examined decision making, which Young and Wilmott claim is also shared. Hardill found that men use their superior earning power to dominate the major decision making within families with regard to moving home, buying a house or car and so on. However, Crompton (1997) argues that as women's earning power increases relative to men's, so men do more in the home and women are more likely to share decision making. However, in 2015 most women earned lots less than men and consequently the division of labour and decision making in the home is likely to remain unequal.

e It is good to see evaluation of the evaluation in this paragraph and a sober informed conclusion as to the immediate future.

It is likely that inequalities in the domestic division of labour persist for a number of reasons. Functionalists believe these differences are natural because they are biological. Feminists believe that they are the product of patriarchal ideology and that female children are persuaded to accept these roles from a very early age because gender role socialisation focuses on toys like dolls and domestic things like cookers for girls. Marxist-feminists blame capitalism and argue that capitalism does little to encourage equality in the home because employers need workers and they need women to give birth to the future workforce. However, Hakim rejects all these areas and actually suggests that some women are happy with inequality in the home because they want to be full-time mothers and housewives. She argues that women are happy to give more commitment to family and children than men. She criticises feminists for seeing the mother–housewife role as having less status than having a career.

ⓔ This section contains both the best and worst of the response to the question. On a positive note, it covers a wide range of theories — functionalism, feminism, Marxist-feminism and the rational choice theory of Hakim — and it is obvious that the student understands them. However, each is dealt with a little too quickly and some crucial points go undeveloped and unevaluated.

ⓔ Overall, however, this is a reasonably sophisticated response. In terms of knowledge and understanding, the student demonstrates excellent knowledge and understanding of the debate, and constructs a logical and persuasive view against the argument embodied in the essay title. All the information presented is relevant and expertly applied. The student is awarded the full 6 marks for this skill. In terms of application, the full 4 marks are awarded because the response is wide ranging and focuses on a variety of theories and studies. In terms of analysis and evaluation, despite the slight disappointment of the final paragraph and the omission of any reference to domestic violence, the student consistently displays the ability to intelligently evaluate throughout the response. For AO3, therefore, 9 marks out of a possible 10 are awarded. **19/20 marks awarded.**

ⓔ **Total score for Section B: 44/45 marks**

ⓔ **Total score for Paper 1: 74/75 marks**

AS question 2

Socialisation, culture and identity

Read the source material and answer questions 1-4.

 Sociologists note that ethnic identity is important to significant numbers of people in the UK. This identity may be based on shared descent, history, language, religion, traditions and so on. However, there is evidence that some British people are adopting mixing and matching elements of different subcultures, especially ethnic ones, in terms of music, dance, fashion, food, education and friendship and therefore creating hybrid identities.

1   Define the concept of hybridity.   (4 marks)

ⓔ Use examples to illustrate your definition.

2   With reference to the source, identify and briefly explain two examples of hybrid identity.   (6 marks)

ⓔ Remember you have both a photograph and text to help explain and illustrate your two examples.

3   Using the source and your wider sociological knowledge, explain how national identity might be shaped by the education system.   (8 marks)

ⓔ Two reasonably detailed paragraphs are required. Do not forget to use the source, e.g. there is a reference to history that could be developed. Examples are crucial to show off your understanding.

4   Explain and briefly evaluate the view that British national identity is in decline.   (12 marks)

ⓔ Begin by explaining what is meant by British national identity and how British people are socialised into it by family, education, media and so on. In the second half of the essay, discuss how recent developments in Scotland and Wales as well as globalisation might be undermining national identity.

Families and relationships

5   Define and briefly explain the difference between a family and a household.   (5 marks)

ⓔ Families are also households so make sure your example of the latter is not family orientated.

6 Identify and briefly describe two recent changes in the relationship between grandparents and grandchildren. (8 marks)

ⓔ Make sure the changes are clearly different from each other.

7 Explain reasons for the decline in marriage since the 1970s. (12 marks)

ⓔ Describe the trends in marriage, showing how trends today compare with the past. However, remember a fall in numbers does not necessarily indicate decline.

8 Evaluate the view that the family is beneficial both for society and for the individual. (20 marks)

ⓔ This is the functionalist argument, which should be outlined in detail and evaluated using Marxist and feminist critiques.

Student answer

1 Hybridity as a concept is normally used in conjunction with the concept of identity. It refers to people mixing and matching elements of more than one culture to create an identity that is unique to them. For example, some British-born Asians may 'borrow' styles or ways of behaving from British culture while retaining and respecting many aspects of their parent culture and religion. Asian men may wear a suit to the wedding of one of their English friends but traditional dress to the wedding of an Asian relative.

ⓔ This is an accurate definition which is well illustrated with examples. **4/4 marks awarded.**

2 The photograph in the source is of a mixed-race family. Such families and their children have grown in numbers in recent years. Platt suggests that children from such families will have hybrid identities because they are likely to be immersed in the two distinct cultures of their parents.

Another example of hybridity in the source is the food that some people eat. When Asians came to the UK in the 1950s they brought their cuisine, particularly curry, with them and many of them opened restaurants. However, some Asian cooks realised that the English were very fond of gravy and invented a dish called tikka masala — a hybrid of Asian curry and English gravy — to cater for English tastes. This is now Britain's favourite dish according to surveys.

ⓔ This shows excellent use of the photograph and a sociological study to illustrate one type of hybridity. The food example is also convincingly discussed in detail. **6/6 marks awarded.**

3 The teaching of history, English literature, English language and religion in British schools tends to promote national identity. For example, Shakespeare is often referred to as the world's greatest playwright while traditional history teaching often focuses on Britain's positive achievements at the expense of such negative British activities as slavery, massacres and exploitation. The Education Reform Act 1988 stresses Christian worship in schools, despite the fact that the UK is a multicultural society.

In 2014 Michael Gove said that schools should promote British values. This was a reaction to accusations that some Islamic schools in Birmingham were promoting values such as intolerance of homosexuals, the segregation of the sexes etc. Some sociologists have argued that the 'hidden curriculum' in schools may result in pupils internalising 'British' values such as fair play, tolerance, equal opportunities etc.

Education is also important in promoting identity because migrants who want to achieve a British identity and citizenship have to pass a 'Life in the UK' test, which consists of 24 questions covering topics such as British values, history, traditions and everyday life. However, critics of this test argue that migrants are expected to know more than English-born citizens probably do.

In Welsh schools, Welsh language and history lessons are a compulsory part of the curriculum even for non-Welsh speakers. Twenty per cent of Welsh children are taught in schools in which Welsh is the first language.

@ This is an excellent response in terms of knowledge and understanding. The student fully understands the debate and uses concepts like values, the hidden curriculum and identity in a confident fashion. The full 4 marks are awarded for this skill. The student is also rewarded with the full 4 marks for application because the response goes beyond a simple discussion of how education promotes national identity. **8/8 marks awarded.**

4   The idea that British national identity is weakening is probably true. There are signs that it is under threat from the Scots and Welsh, who are less likely to feel British today, from multiculturalism because ethnic minorities may be more likely to identify with their ethnic or religious identity, and from globalisation.

According to Guibernau and Goldblatt, British culture and identity were only invented in the eighteenth century after England and Scotland decided to join together. However, today most people are probably able to identify aspects of a distinct and unique British culture or Britishness if asked. Respect for free speech and fair play are seen as essentially British values and drinking tea, playing cricket and queuing as essentially British norms.

However, Waters argues that British culture and identity is under threat and therefore weakening because of four influences. First, there are signs that the Welsh and the Scots (the Celts) are not as committed as the English to Britishness. Most people born in Wales see themselves first and foremost as Welsh rather than British according to one survey. In 2014, 45% of the Scots voted in favour of independence.

Second, Curtice and Heath suggest that 17% of the British population see themselves as English rather than British. These Little Englanders, however, tend to have quite traditional attitudes and consequently tend to be anti-European and anti-immigration. People who vote for UKIP are probably good examples of Little Englanders.

Third, Modood argues that ethnic minorities living in the UK would like to think of themselves as British but are put off by the fact that Little Englanders do not accept their presence in the UK. However, a recent survey carried out by Sunak in 2014 found ethnic minorities were more likely to feel British than white people.

Waters points out that Britishness is mainly being undermined by globalisation. For example, we may work for a multinational company or consume global brands. Globalisation may mean that very little of what we do at work or in our leisure time is 100% British. Global problems such as changes in the world's weather and international terrorism are now our problems.

In conclusion, then, it is probably true that British national identity is weakening today in the UK. There is probably now a new type of global Britishness summed up by the fact that the most popular 'British' food is now chicken tikka masala — a combination of Asian curry and British gravy.

e In terms of knowledge and understanding, the student demonstrates an excellent knowledge of the debate and is able to convincingly support arguments by using a range of sociological studies in depth and detail. The material used is consistently applied to the set question throughout. Perceptive analysis and evaluation is developed throughout the whole response. **12/12 marks awarded.**

e Total score for Section A: 30/30 marks

5 A household consists of a group that shares a common residence such as a family, a student-shared house or flat, pensioners living in sheltered accommodation, a couple and even a single person. People do not have to be related to make up a household. A family on the other hand is composed of a group of people who are related by descent or blood, marriage, adoption and fostering. The family could be nuclear, extended or a stepfamily.

e The student clearly knows the difference between a family and a household, and illustrates those differences confidently. **5/5 marks awarded.**

6 Grandparents today are more healthy and active compared with previous generations and this means that they make more contribution to the socialisation of grandchildren. For example, studies show that 47% of grandparents, especially grandmothers, look after their grandchildren for up to 10 hours a week, saving £11 billion in childcare costs. Grandparents therefore spend more quality time with their grandchildren compared with the past.

Second, Ross found that when grandchildren were younger, grandparents would spend time taking them on outings and playing with them. They also taught them skills. As the grandchildren got older, Ross found that they valued their grandparents because they would give advice and guidance especially if the child was fighting with its parents and financial support. Children felt listened to by their grandparents.

e The student displays excellent knowledge and understanding and presents information and studies that are relevant and substantiated. Full marks are therefore awarded for knowledge and understanding. Application too is focused on the question and consequently another 4 marks are awarded for this skill. **8/8 marks awarded.**

7 Marriage seems to have declined a lot in the UK. For example, in 1972, 480,000 couples got married but in 2009 only 231,000 couples got married. This has led to some New Right sociologists arguing that the decline in marriage is bad for society because marriage is good for social stability and morality. Morgan thinks that all children should be born within the moral framework of marriage. She points out that adultery is still regarded as immoral as a result of the value society puts on marriage.

Morgan blames three things for the decline in marriage: first, the decline in religious beliefs and practices, which means that people no longer see marriage as a sacred thing. Second, cohabitation is increasingly being seen as an alternative to marriage. Third, taxes and the benefits system are not doing enough to encourage marriage.

However, critics argue that marriage is not in decline. It is merely changing. For example, women used to get married for the first time around the age of 22–23 but the average is now 30–31. Wilkinson argues that young women today weigh up the costs of marriage against the benefits of having a career and economic independence and decide to postpone marriage until their careers are established. However, women are not against marriage. The majority of women in the UK are married by the age of 40.

British Social Attitudes survey results consistently show that for both men and women, marriage is the gold standard. Beaujouan found that people only cohabited because they wanted to marry their partner eventually and cohabitation was a good way of working out if marriage would work in practice. Beaujouan actually argues that cohabitation is good for marriage and may have helped bring down the divorce rate.

Finally, the idea that marriage is in decline can also be criticised by examining the number of remarriages, which now total 40% of all marriages. Also, over two-thirds of families in the UK are headed by a married couple. Nearly 60% of these marriages are successful. Marriage is therefore not sick and dying as the New Right claim. It is actually very healthy.

e This student demonstrates an excellent grasp of the debate about marriage and displays range and depth in terms of knowledge and understanding. Sociological evidence in the form of statistical trends and studies is presented in a confident fashion and consequently the full 8 marks are awarded for this skill. Knowledge is applied to the question in an explicit way and so the student is awarded a further 4 marks for this skill. **12/12 marks awarded.**

8 The idea that family is beneficial or functional for both society and the individual is a functionalist one. Functionalists argue the nuclear family is the most important social institution in society because it performs vital functions which are beneficial for family members and for society because it helps bring about value consensus and social order.

Murdock studied 250 societies across the world and claimed on the basis of this that the nuclear family — biological parents in a socially acceptable heterosexual relationship plus children — was universal, i.e. found in all societies. He claimed that the nuclear family effectively performs four crucial functions for society and the individual.

First, he notes that procreation/reproduction ensures the survival of the human group or society over time, and reinforces the marital relationship because the child is a symbol of a couple's love for each other. Second, the sexual function ensures social control and order (e.g. a sexual free-for-all would result in chaos for society) while reinforcing the couple's love for each other. Third, the economic function ensures the survival of children because they are physically and economically dependent on parents for several years. It is also good for society because people learn skills and become workers and contribute to the economic system. Fourth, the educational function is good for individuals because children learn the rules of their culture and how to get along with each other. It is good for society because children learn how to be good conformist citizens.

e These opening paragraphs display excellent knowledge and understanding of the functionalist theory of the family and the material is confidently applied to the question in an explicit way.

Talcott Parsons argues the nuclear family is the family structure best equipped to meet the need of industrial society for a mobile workforce. Parsons argues that the modern nuclear family specialises today in two essential functions which benefit both society and the individual. The first function is 'primary socialisation', which refers to parents teaching their children the basic values and norms of our culture such as gender roles so that children grow up to be good citizens who conform to the rules of society. Parsons sees families as 'personality factories' manufacturing children who grow up to be responsible law-abiding adults.

The second function is the 'stabilisation of the adult personality' — Parsons argues that the family functions like a warm bath to sooth away the everyday stresses and anxieties of living and working in a highly pressured society. In these ways, the isolated nuclear family is functional (beneficial) both for the individual and for industrial modern society.

ⓔ Excellent and relevant knowledge is displayed in these two paragraphs, which address the question in a convincing fashion.

> However, Marxists and feminists reject functionalist assumptions about who benefits from the family. Feminists such as Stanko argue that it paints too rosy a picture of family life and that it ignores the dysfunctions or dark side of family life such as child abuse and domestic violence. Family life therefore is not always beneficial for individuals. Feminists such as Craig also argue that the nuclear family generally oppresses women because they are overwhelmingly responsible for childcare and housework even when they have full-time careers.
>
> Marxists see the family as benefiting the ruling class rather than society as a whole — Benston argues that the future labour force is produced free of charge by mothers, the current male workforce is maintained in a healthy condition by women and children are socialised into values and norms, which means they will grow up to be conformist and uncritical citizens and workers.
>
> Finally, postmodernist thinkers such as Stacey note that the functionalist model of the family implies that other types of family are deviant and cannot perform functions such as socialisation quite as well as the nuclear unit. They also question the idea that the nuclear family is still dominant and point out that family diversity is now the norm. There are lots of other family types in the UK such as one-parent families, reconstituted families and gay/lesbian families which are just as effective as the nuclear unit. Some postmodernists even believe that families no longer have to be related to one another. For example, Heath believes that friendship networks and households can be just as important as family relationships.

ⓔ The final three paragraphs display an excellent ability to analyse and evaluate. There is a range of explicit and detailed points illustrated by sociological studies which clearly address the question. The student is awarded the full 6 marks for a very creditable level of knowledge and understanding, the full 4 marks for the way that the material is always focused on the question and the full 10 marks for a considered and intelligent analysis and evaluation. **20/20 marks awarded.**

ⓔ **Total score for Section B: 45/45 marks**

ⓔ **Total score for Paper 1: 75/75 marks**

AS question 3

Socialisation, culture and identity

Read the source material and answer questions 1–4.

Many sociologists agree that the UK is a class-based society. This means that people are aware of how their job, income and so on shapes their sense of identity as well as their cultural lifestyle. For example, upper-class people have a completely different set of values and enjoy a very different educational and leisure experience compared with people from working-class backgrounds. However, postmodernists argue that class identities are no longer important today.

1 Define the concept of 'cultural capital'. (4 marks)

e Illustrate your answer with examples of cultural capital in practice.

2 With reference to the source, identify and briefly explain **two** examples of how upper-class cultural lifestyles might differ from those experienced by the working classes. (6 marks)

e Use both types of source — one highlights a distinctly upper-class sport while the other highlights leisure (although you will need to provide a specific example).

3 Using the source and your wider sociological knowledge, explain how upper-class identity may differ from working-class identity. (8 marks)

e Show how upper-class identity is composed of specific values and norms and how these are transmitted through the family and education. Contrast this with a similar analysis of working-class identity.

4 Explain and briefly evaluate the view that disabled people's identity is different to that of able-bodied people. (12 marks)

e Traditionally it was assumed that the disabled identity was forged mainly by the person's impairment but most of this essay should explore the idea that disabled people's identity is shaped by disablism.

Families and relationships

5 Define and briefly explain the idea of serial monogamy. (5 marks)

e The brief explanation should focus on why serial monogamy has become more popular.

6 Identify and briefly describe two changes in the fertility rate. (8 marks)

ⓔ Focus on changes in the fertility rates of particular age groups and/or migrants.

7 Explain reasons for the rise in the number of single-parent families. (12 marks)

ⓔ Outline the trends and identify at least four reasons why such families are growing in number.

8 Evaluate the view that family diversity is the norm today. (20 marks)

ⓔ The view is postmodern. You should identify the different types of families that have appeared in recent years and explain the reasons for their growing popularity.

Student answer

1 Cultural capital is a concept developed by the Marxist sociologist Bourdieu and refers to the attitudes, ways of thinking, knowledge and language skills learned in middle-class homes that give middle-class children an advantage over working-class kids in school. For example, middle-class children are more likely to be enrolled at libraries, are more likely to have parents who take them to visit museums and art galleries and are therefore more likely to have more general knowledge than working-class children. They have also spent more time in the company of adults so they know how to respond to teachers.

ⓔ Excellent knowledge is displayed in terms of identifying the source of the concept and its explanation, which is very well developed in terms of the illustration used to convey understanding. **4/4 marks awarded.**

---

2 According to the source, there may be differences in the sports played and watched by the upper class compared with the working class. For example, the upper class play sports such as lacrosse, rugby union, tennis and cricket at their independent schools. Working-class children are more likely to be playing football. When they become adults, the upper class may hunt foxes or go shooting. The source shows the game of polo, which is very expensive and therefore can only be afforded by the upper class.

There are other leisure activities which are distinctly upper class or working class. The upper class may like high culture — for example, going to the opera or ballet or theatre, while the working class prefer television or going to the cinema. The upper class may read *The Times* while the working class are more likely to read the *Sun* or the *Daily Mirror*.

ⓔ The student correctly identifies two cultural lifestyles enjoyed by the upper class and illustrates them in detail with appropriate and explicit examples. **6/6 marks awarded.**

3 Scott points out that the top 7% of the population (the upper class) control most of the wealth of the UK and this allows them to practise social closure — this means they segregate themselves from other social groups such as the working class through the use of intermarriage and by sending their children to expensive and exclusive public schools which are not affordable for working-class people.

Upper-class identity is also distinctive in its use of high culture. These are products or activities that are defined as superior in their creativity compared with popular culture. For example, products such as art, sculpture, antiques and Shakespeare plays, media such as *The Times* newspaper and sporting events such as Henley and Royal Ascot tend to be associated with upper-class identity. In contrast, studies of the working class suggest that they are more likely to enjoy popular cultural pursuits such as watching television, going to the cinema and watching football.

ℯ Excellent detailed knowledge of upper-class identity is demonstrated with perceptive use of concepts and sociological studies to convey understanding. There is explicit and focused application. **8/8 marks awarded.**

4 There are two main factors which affect the identity of the 10 million disabled people in the UK. First, there is a medical model of disability which sees a disabled person's identity as an aspect of their impairment. Doctors, for example, might not treat a disabled person as an ordinary person who just happens to have a disability. Instead the disabled person is defined and treated in terms of what they cannot do and as dependent on their able-bodied carers. It is just assumed that disabled people cannot lead independent lives.

However, sociologists like Tom Shakespeare argue that the danger in this is that such labels can result in a self-fulfilling prophecy. It is argued that if disabled people are constantly subjected to the view that they are dependent, weak, abnormal and have little status, the disabled individual may actually take on a 'disabled identity' in order to interact successfully with doctors, social workers, the general public and so on.

The social model of disability, on the other hand, which is argued by disabled sociologists like Shakespeare and Barnes, claims that this dependent identity is caused by society's prejudices and fears about disability. As a result of these, disabled people are defined as abnormal or deviant by society while disability is regarded as something to be avoided at all costs.

Shakespeare therefore argues that disabled individuals are actually disabled by society. Hyde agrees and argues that people with impairments are excluded by a social environment which is inaccessible and discriminatory. For example, disabled people are often prevented from travelling to work, not by their inability to use buses, but because public transport has been designed for the exclusive use of able-bodied people. Oliver concludes that the disadvantages imposed by society on disabled people are at least as great as those imposed by the disability.

ⓔ This response displays an excellent knowledge and understanding of the notion of a disabled identity and intelligently develops this theme through its identification of the two approaches and its illustrative use of concepts such as the self-fulfilling prophecy and reference to studies such as Shakespeare and Barnes. The material used is always relevant and focused on the question. The evaluation of the medical model is first class but evaluation of the social model is also needed. The student is awarded 4 marks for knowledge, 4 marks for application and 3 marks for evaluation. **11/12 marks awarded.**

ⓔ Total score for Section A: 29/30 marks

> **5** This concept refers to the idea that people during the course of their lifetime are likely to have a series of monogamous long-term relationships which may result in more than one cohabitation and marriage. It has now replaced monogamy or marriage to one person for life. The idea of marriage for life has been undermined by the availability of divorce, the decline of religion and changing attitudes especially among women who are no longer willing to put up with unhappy empty-shell marriages.

ⓔ The student is awarded full marks because the response is excellent in its use of an accurate and detailed definition which encompasses both marriage and cohabitation and is focused on contrasting serial monogamy with monogamy. Relevant and accurate reasons are also offered as illustration. **5/5 marks awarded.**

> **6** In the twenty-first century, women are delaying having families compared with the past. Changes in fertility rates suggest that women are having children at an older age than they were 30 years ago. In general, fertility rates for women aged 30 and above have increased, while those for women aged below 30 have declined. The number of children born to women aged 40 and over has doubled in the last 20 years.
>
> In recent years, the UK has experienced a rise in fertility which has been credited to immigration and the increase in the number of mothers born overseas. These migrants are more likely to be young and of childbearing age. Babies born to mothers from overseas now account for over a quarter of all births in the UK.

ⓔ Excellent, well-illustrated and relevant knowledge is demonstrated of two changes in the fertility rate. **8/8 marks awarded.**

> **7** In 1961, only 2% of all UK households were made up of single-parent families. In 2012 there were 2 million such households making up about a quarter of all families in the UK. About 3 million children lived in such families in 2012.

Ninety per cent of single-parent families are headed by women. Most of these are ex-married but are now divorced, separated or widowed. The fastest-growing group of single parents is made up of those who have never married or cohabited. Haskey estimated this group to be a quarter of all single mothers.

New Right thinkers like Charles Murray blame what they call 'perverse incentives' for the rise in single mothers. He argues that welfare benefits are too generous and this is encouraging teenage girls to get pregnant and to live off the state.

However, feminist sociologists point out that only 3% of unmarried mothers are teenagers. The average age of a single mother in the UK is 34 according to the National Council for One-Parent Families. Second, there is little evidence in support of the view that young women are deliberately getting pregnant to get benefits. Ford and Millar note that many single mothers experience poverty, debt and material hardship despite being on benefits.

Feminists also argue that changes in fertility suggest that some older successful career women are choosing to have and to bring up children alone. However, these women are rarely referred to as a problem by the New Right because they cost the state nothing.

Finally, it is important to remember that statistics only give us a snapshot picture of one moment in time. Single parents may find a new partner and marry them or cohabit with them. The child will then end up living in a reconstituted nuclear family with two parents.

ⓔ A wide range of knowledge is demonstrated which clearly shows that the student understands the reasons why the number of one-parent families has increased and the sociological debate between the New Right and feminists. There is good use of sociological evidence — Haskey, Ford and Millar etc. The line of reasoning is clear and all the material is focused on the question. **12/12 marks awarded.**

8   New Right sociologists argue that the nuclear family is the best type of family to live in but they also argue that it is under attack from trends such as divorce, cohabitation, falls in the birth and fertility rates etc. However, in contrast, postmodernists argue that these factors are generally positive because they have contributed to family diversity — a range of alternative family arrangements which mean that the nuclear family may no longer be the norm.

Postmodernist sociologists argue that there now exist a greater choice and variety than ever before in terms of family lifestyles. The Rapaports, for example, note family life is now characterised by structural diversity — in addition to the married or cohabiting nuclear family, the UK has seen dramatic growth in the one-parent family, which makes up nearly a quarter of all UK families and about 50% of African-Caribbean families. Divorce is probably the main cause of this type of family. However, single parents often remarry (40% of all marriages are remarriages) and consequently the reconstituted or stepfamily is also increasing in number. These can be quite complex in terms of their co-parenting arrangements and children often find themselves active members of two nuclear families. There are now also same-sex families in that gay people can get married and adopt children.

🄴 These first two paragraphs set the context for the theoretical debate between the New Right and postmodernism and clearly demonstrate a good knowledge and understanding of each position. With regard to family diversity, an excellent range of alternative family types is identified and explained.

The population of the UK is ageing because of increased life expectancy and falls in both the birth rate and the fertility rate and this has led to a rise in the number of extended families as children increasingly care for elderly kin. Some sociologists such as O'Brien and Jones suggest that living in the same area can also qualify kin as an extended unit especially if there is regular contact and a strong sense of duty and obligation to each other.

Julia Brannen has also identified beanpole families in which grandparents play a major role in looking after their grandchildren. They may also be involved in looking after their own very elderly parents. The ageing of the population has also led to an increase in the number of elderly single-person households. Many of these are widows because women live longer than men.

🄴 This section demonstrates a strong understanding of how the ageing of the British population has impacted on family diversity. References to sociological studies are detailed and accurate.

There is also cultural diversity in family life. Global migration has resulted in the UK becoming a multicultural society. Most Asians and African-Caribbeans live in nuclear families although internal arrangements may differ from white nuclear families. About a third of Asian families are extended, e.g. Sikhs are more likely to live in horizontal extended families of brothers and their wives. There has also been a great deal of intermarriage between whites, African-Caribbeans and Chinese, which has resulted in a dramatic increase in mixed-race children.

🄴 Excellent knowledge of the effect of global migration on family diversity is demonstrated.

Finally, some postmodernists have drawn attention to the increasing importance of young single-person households which are also on the increase. Many of these are composed of professional career women who have postponed marriage and family life in favour of independence. In addition, postmodernist sociologists like Smart argue that sociologists should study 'personal life' rather than family because newer types of relationships such as same-sex relationships, relationships in which people commit to each other but live apart from one another, open relationships and friendships may be becoming more important than family relationships in the twenty-first century.

e This evaluative section is very sophisticated and clearly shows a strong grasp of postmodern thinking on family diversity.

However, Chester argues that postmodernists exaggerate the importance of family diversity because most adults still marry and have children. Most children are reared by their natural parents. Most people live in a household shared by a married couple. Most marriages continue until parted by death. However, the increasing number of other family types cannot be ignored and probably indicates a slow but steady drift away from the nuclear ideal towards family diversity.

e These conclusions are reflective and make pertinent evaluative observations about the postmodern position.

e Overall, this student clearly understands the debate and consequently the content of this essay is substantiated, accurate and detailed, and always focused on the question in an analytical and evaluative way. The student is therefore awarded 6 marks for knowledge and understanding, 4 marks for application and the full 10 marks for evaluation. **20/20 marks awarded.**

e Total score for Section B: 45/45 marks

e Total score for Paper 1: 74/75 marks

■ The A-level examination

The topics of socialisation, culture and identity and the option 'Families and relationships' are examined on Paper 1 of the A-level examination, **Socialisation, culture and identity**. The questions on socialisation, culture and identity appear in Section A of Paper 1 as questions 1–3. These are a mixture of short, medium and extended compulsory questions. Some are based on source material. Section A questions add up to 38 marks altogether, or 42% of the paper.

The three questions on families and relationships appear in Section B, Option 1 as questions 4–6. These are a mixture of medium and extended compulsory questions. Section B questions add up to 52 marks altogether, or 58% of the paper.

The whole exam lasts for 1 hour 30 minutes, carries 90 marks and is worth 30% of the A-level qualification. It is worth spending about 40 minutes on Section A and 50 minutes on Section B. Try to manage your time so that you have enough spare to read through your responses to the whole paper at the end.

A-level question 1

Socialisation, culture and identity

1 **Explain, using examples, the concept of popular culture.** (6 marks)

🅔 Do not forget to illustrate with examples.

Source A

Source B

In addition to the family, a range of other social institutions are involved in socialisation. These secondary agents of socialisation include old and new forms of mass media, the educational system, religion and the peer group.

2 Using Sources A and B and your wider sociological knowledge, explain the concept of secondary socialisation.

(12 marks)

ⓔ You should aim to write a side of A4 which defines secondary socialisation and illustrate the concept using education, the media and so on.

3 Outline and briefly evaluate the view that there have been major changes in gender identity in the last 40 years.

(20 marks)

ⓔ Before you can discuss these changes, you need to describe what gender identity was like 40 years ago.

Family and relationships

4 Outline two reasons for the increase in cohabitation and illustrate your answer with examples.

(12 marks)

ⓔ Two detailed paragraphs are required.

5 Explain and briefly evaluate the view that British society is child-centred. (16 marks)

ⓔ Explain why childhood is seen as a special state and how parents and the state attempt to ensure this. Evaluate by looking at the dark side of family life.

6 Assess the view that gender roles and relationships have become more equal in modern family life.

(24 marks)

ⓔ Outline Young and Wilmott's ideas about the symmetrical family and use a range of feminist studies to show that equality has not yet been achieved.

| Student answer |

1 Popular culture mainly refers to the products of the mass media such as television programmes, films, magazines and comics and pop music. It is sometimes called mass culture because it is manufactured for the mass or majority of a society to consume and enjoy. It is often written off as having little or no artistic merit compared with high culture such as classic literature and plays written by Shakespeare, which are seen as having more creative status and associated with the upper class.

Many critical sociologists are critical of popular culture. For example, some see it as corrupting young people while Marxists see it as an ideological means of distracting the poor from critical thought. If people become obsessed with *Coronation Street* or *Big Brother* they are unlikely to be thinking critically about inequalities in wealth or power or the unfairness of austerity cuts.

ⓔ An accurate explanation of popular culture is offered and the student shows excellent ability in comparing it with high culture and then discussing why it is criticised by some sociologists, notably Marxists. **6/6 marks awarded.**

2 Socialisation is the process by which we learn the culture of our society. The primary agent of socialisation is the family. As the source indicates, secondary agents include education, religion, the peer group as well as old forms of media such as television and newspapers and new forms which the picture source suggests are internet based such as social network sites such as Facebook.

Education is a very important agency of socialisation because most children will spend at least 11 years in schools and colleges. The functionalist thinker Durkheim argued that education is essential because it socialises children into the key values of our society — achievement, competition and individualism, resulting in value consensus. It also promotes a sense of belonging to society by linking the individual to society through the study of history.

However, Marxists have a much more negative view of education as an agency of socialisation. Althusser argues that education is a tool of the capitalist class because it is dominated by an invisible 'hidden curriculum' — a set of ruling-class ideas that encourages conformity and unquestioning acceptance of hierarchy, inequality and capitalism.

Another important secondary agent of socialisation is the mass media, which are made up of television, advertising, newspapers, magazines, films, music, the internet etc. Postmodernists argue that the media provide people with positive role models and a sense of identity through internet social networking sites such as Twitter, Instagram and Facebook.

Marxists, however, see the influence of the media as a bad thing because they are manufactured to keep the masses happy by encouraging them to buy into capitalism by investing in 'false needs' and popular culture such as television soap operas. Any serious thought or criticism is discouraged. Marxists call this false class consciousness.

Religion is another secondary agent of socialisation and Durkheim argued that the major function of religion is to socialise people into special or sacred values known as moral codes. Marxists, on the other hand, believe that religion merely distracts us from the problems that are caused by capitalism.

Finally, functionalists are anxious about peer groups because membership of these may exert a strong influence over adolescent behaviour and attitudes, and create tension/conflict between children and parents. It may also create crime and deviance as peers are pressured to engage in antisocial behaviour such as bullying.

ⓔ This answer demonstrates an excellent understanding of a range of agents of secondary socialisation and the debates surrounding their function. The source material is acknowledged and used effectively. The material is generally accurate and focused on sociological theory in a convincing way. The student is therefore awarded 4 marks for knowledge and understanding and a further 8 marks for application because material used is both relevant and consistently applied to the question. **12/12 marks awarded.**

---

3   Many sociologists, especially postmodernists, have argued that significant social and economic changes have occurred in the last 40 years which have led to major changes in the role and identity of women and men. It is suggested that the choices available to females today have increased and consequently they are less likely to subscribe to hegemonic definitions of femininity. As Sharpe argues, young women no longer see getting married and having children as their priority. Similarly, young men are changing too in that, according to Whannel, they are less likely to believe in traditional versions of masculinity focused on being tough but are now more willing to explore their feminine side.

ⓔ This is a good introduction which sets the scene for the debate about gender change.

Feminine identity has undergone major change because of social, economic, political and cultural factors, e.g. the economy and work have become feminised in the last 40 years according to Wilkinson. The decline of the male-dominated manufacturing sector and the rise in the female-dominated service sector, especially retail and finance, has meant that women today have many more opportunities for careers, especially in management and the professions. They are no longer expected to solely occupy the mother–housewife role and work for 'pin money'.

It is argued by feminist sociologists such as Sharpe and Lees that young women today are much more assertive and are increasingly expecting their identity to be wrapped up with their career and work rather than domestic roles. They are now more likely to be economically independent and may even be the main breadwinner in periods of high male unemployment. In education, we can see that females are outperforming males and surveys such as that conducted by Sharpe in the mid-1990s suggest that female priorities have changed dramatically from the 1960s when they were focused on boyfriends, marriage and children. Women now want careers and some young women are choosing voluntary childlessness in order to concentrate on this.

ⓔ Good knowledge of a range of studies is demonstrated in these two paragraphs about how and why feminine identity may have changed.

However, not all feminists are convinced. Delamont, for example, argues that these changes and choices have been exaggerated and consequently hegemonic definitions are still firmly in place. In particular, although more women have moved into the workforce, men still dominate top jobs and women on average are still paid less than men. Men still dominate management and professional jobs. Oakley points out that women are still labouring under a dual burden, i.e. they hold down jobs yet still take the major responsibility for childcare and housework. Hakim also points out that there is still a great deal of pressure on women to become wives and mothers. Socialisation into gender roles in families is also still very traditional, e.g. girls are given dolls and domestic toys, which helps prepare them for a very different future to boys. Wolf points out that women too are judged by the media in terms of their beauty, sexiness, size, shape etc. and this leads to some girls becoming anorexic or bulimic.

ⓔ An excellent evaluative paragraph questions change from a range of angles using a good variety of sociological studies.

Some sociologists argue that men are undergoing change too. Economic recession linked to globalisation, the decline in manufacturing industry, the fact that most new jobs are for women and the resulting rise in male unemployment has had dramatic consequences for traditional masculinity. Working-class men have found their masculinity challenged by the humiliation of being unemployed. O'Donnell suggests men are experiencing a crisis of masculinity and believes that social problems such as domestic violence, male suicide rates and underachievement are caused by this. Whannel documents the emergence of alternative types of masculinity in recent years such as the metrosexual, who combines both masculine and feminine characteristics, e.g. David Beckham, the hipster movement, which it is argued is more sensitive to the needs of females, and gay subculture.

ⓔ Excellent knowledge and understanding is demonstrated of changes in masculinity. The student confidently uses a range of sociological sources.

Finally, in conclusion, some sociologists have noted that these changes have benefited middle-class white men and women rather than working-class white, Asian or African-Caribbean men and women, who may find their choices are restricted by poverty, tradition and religion. Some ethnic subcultures may even feel threatened by these gendered changes because they have subscribed to very traditional notions of dominant masculinity and subordinate femininity for thousands of years. This may mean that they actively resist the possibility of such change.

ⓔ This response has been evaluative in tone throughout but this paragraph comprises some very perceptive evaluation about gendered change and how it may be undermined by class and ethnicity.

e Overall, this student has demonstrated excellent knowledge and understanding throughout and has utilised an impressive array of sociological evidence in terms of sociological studies. The information presented is both relevant and substantial, and therefore the student is awarded the full 8 marks for this skill. Applications skills are also excellent. All the material is intelligently related to the question. The full 8 marks are therefore awarded for this skill. Full marks are also awarded for analysis and evaluation, which is apparent throughout. **20/20 marks awarded.**

e Total score for Section A: 38/38 marks

> **4**　About a quarter of all men and women will live with someone outside of marriage at some point. The New Right see cohabitation as inferior and immoral compared with marriage. They argue that it is increasingly replacing marriage. Morgan calls it marriage-lite because she believes it does not involve the commitment that marriage demands. However, the evidence from British Social Attitudes surveys shows that few people see cohabitation as an alternative to marriage. Beaujohan's research found that marriage is still regarded as the gold standard by the majority of people. Most couples therefore cohabit as a dress rehearsal for marriage — as a test of compatibility and marriage-worthiness. Cohabitation has therefore increased because people want their marriages to be successful. Most successful cohabitation is eventually converted into marriage.
>
> The increase in cohabitation may also reflect other social trends. For example, religious beliefs once stressed the sinfulness of living together outside of marriage. However, religious beliefs have declined — a process known as secularisation. Consequently, moral disapproval of cohabitation, especially from extended kin and the community, is no longer as powerful as it was in the past. However, cohabitation is not popular in ethnic minority communities because religious controls are still quite powerful. It is generally something quite unique to secular communities.

e The student demonstrates an excellent knowledge and understanding of the reasons for the increase in cohabitation. A range of sociological material is used — theories such as the New Right and the British Social Attitudes survey. All the material is applied consistently to the question. **12/12 marks awarded.**

> **5**　Functionalist or 'March of Progress' sociologists have suggested that the modern family has become more child-centred over the course of the last century. Aries, for example, claims that in preindustrial society, childhood as we know it today did not exist. Children were 'little adults' who took part in the same work on the land as adults as soon as they were physically able, i.e. at the age of 4. Even after industrialisation, working-class children were sent into the factories, mines and mills, in which they worked very long hours. Many were killed and injured doing this work.

Aries argues that middle-class attitudes towards childhood started to change towards the middle of the nineteenth century. Children were banned from working in factories, mills and mines in the 1860s (although the working classes strongly opposed this because of the loss of income), mass compulsory education was introduced in the 1880s and a legal age of consent was introduced to protect children from sexual predators.

Cunningham argues that the twentieth century saw a major shift in social attitudes towards childhood, which produced a 'child-centred society'. This means that the world of childhood was seen for the first time as separate to the world of adulthood. Today, children are seen as vulnerable and dependent on adults for both protection and economic welfare, especially by the state. Children are viewed as having the right to happiness and play.

Furthermore, the state has taken responsibility for ensuring that parents and other agencies treat children well and there are several laws and social policies which aim to protect children's rights, e.g. the 2004 Children's Act declares that 'Every Child Matters' and that all children have a right to be healthy and to stay safe.

However, neglect and child abuse are still common occurrences. For example, one child in the UK loses its life every week according to the NSPCC at the hands of a parent. New Right sociologists such as Postman and Palmer see childhood as under threat because television exposes children too soon to the adult world. Postman believes that the media have become more influential than parents and have encouraged young girls to see themselves as sexual beings at a much younger age. Palmer argues that electronic technologies such as television, computer games and the internet are being used by parents as alternatives to traditional parenting practices. Instead of spending quality time with their children and reading them stories, Palmer claims parents are too happy to use television, electronic games and junk food to keep them quiet. Children are therefore deprived of traditional childhood and family life, and she claims that every year children become more antisocial — less able to learn, to enjoy life and to thrive socially — because of these trends.

(e) The student demonstrates an excellent knowledge and understanding of a range of sociological material about childhood which is generally accurate, detailed and relevant. The material is consistently and frequently related to the question. Analysis and evaluation are sustained throughout but especially in the debate about threats to childhood today. Full marks are awarded for each of the three skills. **16/16 marks awarded.**

6   Functionalist sociologists such as Parsons and Young and Wilmott have argued that changing attitudes to gender roles and increased participation by women in the labour market have led to more equality in modern family life. Parsons argued that men and women performed separate roles within the family and these were 'equal but different'.

Wilmott and Young invented the concept of the symmetrical nuclear family in which, they argued, equality in marriage was now the norm. They claimed that the relationship between husband and wife (the conjugal relationship) was becoming more joint, meaning that wives were now going out to work and men were more likely to share childcare, housework, decision making and leisure time with their wives. This trend towards egalitarian marriage, Wilmott and Young claimed, was caused by the decline in the extended family, and the increasing opportunities in paid employment for women.

e The student rightly and intelligently contextualises the debate by outlining studies which argued that roles and relationships were now more equal in terms of domestic responsibilities within families. It is important to do this because it is this position that the rest of the essay is going to question. You cannot knock something down unless you have built it up in the first place.

However, feminist sociologists strongly oppose the idea that modern marriages are characterised by equality. Oakley's study of housewives in the 1970s found that only 15% of husbands had a high level of participation in housework and only 25% had a high participation in childcare. More modern data suggest little has changed. Research by Craig (2007) found that women do between one-third and one-half more housework than men. She argues that this inequality begins when a couple move in together and before they have children. She calls this aspect of domestic inequality the 'partnership penalty'. Her research found that when couples marry, the wife's unpaid domestic labour rises in volume while the husband does less housework compared with when he was single. Ben-Galim and Thompson (2013) found that eight out of ten married women carried out more household chores than men, while only one in ten married men did an equal amount of cleaning and washing as his wife. In 2014 the BBC found evidence that many couples are in conflict because women are unhappy with the amount of domestic labour being done by their male partners.

e This is a detailed paragraph which demonstrates excellent knowledge of a range of contemporary sociological studies which are relevant to the debate.

Also, women's lives are often characterised by a double shift or burden — this means they work full time and still do most of the housework and childcare. Ferri and Smith surveyed fathers and mothers who both worked full time and found that fathers took the main responsibility for childcare in a tiny number of families. Ramos also found that unemployed men's domestic labour only just matched that of their working wives. Most of these men believed that housework was her responsibility. Duncombe and Marsden argue that women experience a triple shift of labour within families — they work full time, they are mainly responsible for housework and childcare and they emotionally maintain and support other family

> members. Hardill found that men use their superior earning power to dominate the major decision making within families, while Crompton found that the more money a woman earned, the more likely her husband was to do more housework. However, most women earn considerably less than men so equality in housework is still a long way off.

🅮 This section is analytical and evaluative in tone as it explores studies which support the feminist case that contemporary family life is characterised by inequalities in gender roles and relationships.

> Overall, the evidence supports the feminist case that modern marriages are not as equal as functionalists suggest. However, Hakim claims that women have more power than feminists say they do — for example, they can now divorce men who refuse to share domestic responsibilities. Also Hakim points out that many women do not want their partners to share housework or childcare. These women are happy to do this work. Some women are more than happy to support their husband's careers by taking on the bulk of the domestic work. These women therefore rationally and deliberately choose inequality. It is not forced on them by men. Hakim is critical of modern feminism because it fails to see that being a full-time mother is just as important as having a career. She accuses feminism of devaluing the mother–homemaker role.

🅮 This is an excellent paragraph in which the critics of equality are themselves evaluated.

🅮 Overall, this is a very perceptive summary of the debate that demonstrates excellent knowledge and understanding and uses an impressive range and variety of sociological theory, studies and evidence in support. There are some things missing — for example, domestic violence is omitted — but the quality of what is included makes up for that omission. Every aspect of this essay is relevant and focused on addressing the main theme of the essay title. Analysis is reasonably sophisticated and evaluation is not only confined to the final paragraph but interweaved throughout. The student is awarded the full 8 marks for each skill. **24/24 marks awarded.**

🅮 **Total score for Section B: 52/52 marks**

🅮 **Total score for Paper 1: 90/90 marks**

A-level question 2

Socialisation, culture and identity

1 **Explain, using examples, the concept of hegemonic masculinity.**   (6 marks)

ⓔ Do not forget to use examples.

Source A

Chinatown in Liverpool

Source B

A culture can be diverse in several ways. Global migration has led to ethnic and religious diversity in the UK today. Cultural diversity can also come about as distinct subcultures appear based on social class, sexuality, youth and even political affiliation. Many of these are community-based.

2 **Using Sources A and B and your wider sociological knowledge, explain the concept of cultural diversity.**   (12 marks)

ⓔ Define cultural diversity and use ethnicity, youth, politics and sexuality in particular to illustrate it.

3 **Outline and briefly evaluate the view that ethnicity plays a significant part in the construction of identity.**   (20 marks)

ⓔ Outline in some detail how ethnicity shapes identity. Evaluate using the concepts of hybridity, globalisation and regional identity.

Family and relationships

4 **Outline two reasons for the increase in divorce and illustrate your answer with examples.** (12 marks)

ⓔ Choose two very different reasons.

5 **Explain and briefly evaluate the view that the modern family is dysfunctional.** (16 marks)

ⓔ Dysfunctional means harmful or bad. Begin with a contrast — a brief mention of functionalism, which sees nuclear families as beneficial, and then discuss the dark side of family life and the feminist critiques of the family.

6 **Assess the Marxist theory of the family.** (24 marks)

ⓔ Outline the ideas of Zaretsky in detail as well as Marxist-feminism. Evaluate using functionalism, feminism and interactionism.

Student answer

1 This concept refers to a very traditional set of ideas about how proper men were supposed to behave in British society. These ideas, which said that men should be the main family breadwinners and heads of the household, were very popular in British culture. They also said that men and boys should not show their emotions. Instead Connell argues men were expected to be emotionally and physically tough and rational in thought.

These ideas are very patriarchal because they imply that women are not equal to men. However, they are now declining in influence as men are encouraged to get in touch with their emotional or feminine side. Alternative types of masculinity — the new man, the metrosexual man, the gay man, the hipster etc. — have become more socially acceptable and popular. However, while Connell accepts that most men do not conform to the image of hegemonic masculinity, they benefit from it in terms of jobs and domestic responsibilities because it is assumed that men should be breadwinners and that they should not have to be mainly responsible for housework and childcare.

ⓔ Excellent knowledge is demonstrated and a sociological study (Connell) is confidently used to support the concept of hegemonic masculinity. The concept is also analysed and illustrated well. **6/6 marks awarded.**

---

2 Cultural diversity refers to cultural differences that exist in societies despite the fact that there is consensus or agreement on fundamental values and norms and that people still experience a common sense of belonging.

Cultural diversity is particularly visible in the neighbourhood make-up of British cities. The picture source of Chinatown tells us that the Chinese have established themselves as a distinct ethnic minority subculture in Liverpool. Other ethnic minority subcultures are associated with particular neighbourhoods, communities and cities. For example, Indians in Leicester, Pakistanis in Bradford, Bangladeshis in Brick Lane and African-Caribbeans in Brixton are all good examples of cultural diversity.

Source B says that global migration has led to cultural diversity in terms of ethnic and religious groups existing alongside each other in a multicultural society. Modood notes that a multicultural society is one in which ethnic and religious diversity is acknowledged and encouraged. Aspects of all cultures — majority and minority — are accepted and celebrated including historical and religious traditions in dress, diet, worship and traditions. The emphasis in multicultural societies is on all ethnic and religious subcultures enjoying the same status and rights, living alongside each other peacefully and respecting one another's beliefs, customs and heritage.

In addition to ethnic and religious diversity, sociologists have also identified cultural diversity based on social class. This might be based on areas. For example, the East End of London is well known for its working-class ties, Bloomsbury and Hampstead are famous for their upper middle-class connections, while Hoxton and Shoreditch in London are notorious for their hipster presence. There are also class differences in cultural and leisure practices. High cultural pursuits including opera, ballet, theatre and so on are seen as middle-class and upper-class pursuits, while going to football matches, watching television and reading tabloid newspapers are seen as part of popular cultural activities enjoyed by the working class.

The source also notes cultural diversity based on sexuality. Gay subcultures can be physically seen in the Gay village of Manchester as well as Brighton. A politically active gay subculture means that gay issues continue to be debated. This may make it easier for other forms of sexuality — for example, transgender — to be accepted by mainstream culture in the future.

Finally, the source notes cultural diversity in terms of politics and youth. Some young people might identify themselves as anarchists or vegetarians while others may identify with youth subcultures such as goths or emos.

ⓔ An excellent knowledge and understanding of the concept of cultural diversity is intelligently illustrated throughout this response. The sources are used extensively. The student is awarded the full 4 marks for knowledge. Only one sociological study is used but this is compensated for by the very good ability shown in the application of sociological concepts such as consensus, multiculturalism, global migration, high culture and popular culture. The content of this response addresses the question throughout. It is therefore awarded 8 marks for this skill. **12/12 marks awarded.**

3   An ethnic group is a social group that shares a common and distinctive culture, religion, language and set of traditions. Ethnicity has a significant effect on identity in the UK today because the UK is a multicultural society and contains a number of ethnic minority groups. Such cultures are still very traditional in terms of their values, lifestyles and identities.

e The student begins well by defining ethnicity and explaining why it is important in a multicultural society.

> Ethnicity is often underpinned by religious beliefs. Modood notes the centrality of religion in Muslim communities in particular and points out that it shapes the lifestyle of Muslim people, particularly in terms of their diet. For example, they will not eat pork products and they can only eat halal-prepared meat. On religious occasions such as Ramadan, they will fast. Religion also shapes other customs and traditions such as dress codes. For example, many Muslim women choose to cover their heads with the hijab. Muslims also practise social closure in that they rarely marry outside their religious group.
>
> Ghuman argues that Asian religions stress that parents should socialise their children to be obedient, and loyal to and respectful of their elders and community around them. Social conformity is demanded and children learn to be interdependent. Asian children too tend to be bilingual, and are often able to use both the mother language, e.g. Urdu, Punjabi, Gujarati and Hindi, and English interchangeably. Ghuman also notes that the choice of marriage partner is thought to be best left to parents (arranged marriage). Family life in Asian culture, therefore, tends to be very different from mainstream culture. Beishon found that Asians, young and old, were very keen on extended family ties and strongly supportive of marriage.

e Excellent knowledge of ethnic identity is demonstrated, using three sociological studies.

> Charlotte Butler studied third-generation young Muslim women and found that they choose from a variety of possible identities. Some will choose to reflect their ethnic and religious identities through the wearing of traditional dress, while others may take a more 'negotiated' position. This may mean adopting Western forms of identity when considering education, careers, domestic roles and equality while retaining some respect for traditional religious ideas about the role of women. These different types of identity may result in conflict between the older and younger generations according to Modood.
>
> Johal's research focused on second- and third-generation British Asians and found that they have a dual or hybrid identity in that they inherit an Asian identity and adopt a British one. This results in Asian youth adopting a 'white mask' in order to interact with white peers at school or college, but emphasising their cultural difference whenever they feel it is necessary. This again supports the view that cultural diversity rather than similarity is the norm in the UK today.

e Excellent knowledge of how ethnic identities may be changing is demonstrated, using sociological evidence.

> However, there are other important ethnic identities in the UK. There are big Jewish communities in London and Leeds. There are sizeable Polish, African-Caribbean, Chinese and African communities. In London alone, there are over 50 ethnic minority communities and 300 languages spoken.
>
> However, in some parts of the country regional or national identities overlap with ethnic identities. For example, Waters argues that Celtic identity is important in Scotland and Wales, while Curtice argues that some English people subscribe to a Little Englander identity in that they are anti-Europe and anti-immigration.
>
> Finally, postmodernist sociologists argue that globalisation is having an effect on young people across all ethnic groups and creating hybrid identities. Young people are now likely to share global tastes in fashion, music, food, drink etc. However, we must be careful not to exaggerate these similarities — traditional ethnic identities, especially in terms of religious influence on lifestyle, still remain the norm. Ethnicity is also influenced by social class. Middle-class Asians may have completely different ideas about their ethnic identity compared with poorer working-class Asian people.

e The above paragraphs contain some creditable evaluation focused on national and regional identity. The impact of globalisation is also considered.

e Overall, the student demonstrates excellent knowledge and understanding of a range of sociological material about ethnic identity. The sociological studies and evidence cited are accurate, detailed and relevant and so the student is awarded 8 marks for knowledge. In terms of application, the material is focused on addressing the question throughout and consequently the student is awarded 8 marks for this skill. The student displays an excellent ability to evaluate and is able to consider a range of influences on the concept of ethnic identity. The student is therefore awarded the full 4 marks for this skill. **20/20 marks awarded.**

e **Total score for Section A: 38/38 marks**

> **4** First, changes in divorce law, especially the introduction of the Divorce Reform Act in 1970, have generally made it easier and cheaper to end marriages. Before this legislation, divorce was expensive and complex. It involved going to court and 'proving' that the spouse was guilty of a matrimonial 'crime' such as adultery. Many people could not afford this legal process and consequently found themselves trapped in unhappy empty-shell marriages. However, the Divorce Reform Act changed the rules and stated that only a 2-year separation (5 years if the other spouse disagreed) was required for a divorce to be granted on the grounds of irretrievable breakdown of marriage. The passing of this Act led to a massive increase in divorce as those previously trapped in empty-shell marriages took advantage of this new law. However, legal changes reflect other changes in society, especially changes in attitudes.

Some sociologists believe that divorce has increased because social expectations about marriage have changed. Functionalist sociologists believe that high divorce rates may be evidence that marriage is increasingly valued and that people are demanding higher standards from their partners. Couples are no longer prepared to put up with unhappy, 'empty-shell' marriages. Similarly, feminist sociologists note that women's expectations of marriage have radically changed, compared with previous generations. In the 1990s most divorce petitions were initiated by women. Thornes and Collard, for example, found that women expect far more from marriage than men. Women may value friendship, emotional gratification, sexual compatibility, companionship and equality more than men do. If husbands fail to live up to these expectations, women may feel the need to look elsewhere.

Women's expectations have probably changed as a result of the improved educational and career opportunities they have experienced since the 1980s. Women no longer have to be unhappily married because they are financially dependent on their husbands.

(e) This student has aimed for about 300 words in the time available and has demonstrated an excellent understanding of two broad reasons for the increase in divorce, using a range of sociological evidence and studies to illustrate. All the information presented is relevant and substantiated. Consequently, 8 marks are awarded for knowledge and 4 marks for application. **12/12 marks awarded.**

5 Functionalist sociologists such as Parsons see the nuclear family as a system of positive loving relationships which meet the basic human need for love and intimacy. It is seen as good for society and positive for the individuals who comprise it.

However, feminists note that most recorded murders, assaults and various types of child abuse take place within the family. One child a week dies at the hands of its parents in the UK. The NSPCC notes that the different types of child abuse are a major social problem. These are probably under-reported because sometimes children do not know they are victims.

Another dysfunction of families in the UK is domestic violence — the power of men to control women by physical force. This type of violence is estimated to be the most common type of violence in Britain. Stanko's survey found that one incident of domestic violence is reported by women to the police every minute in the UK. Mirlees-Black found that 70% of reported domestic violence is violence by men against their female partners.

Feminist sociologists suggest that domestic violence is an aspect of patriarchy and have suggested several explanations for its persistence. First, they note boys are socialised into 'masculine' values which revolve around toughness, aggression, proving oneself etc. Violence for some men may be a product of such socialisation. Second, O'Donnell argues that some men may resort to violence as a result of a crisis of masculinity brought on by unemployment. It is an attempt to reassert their masculinity.

Third, Marxist-feminists such as Ansley and Feeley argue that men's frustration and alienation with capitalism is absorbed by the wife in the form of domestic violence. The powerlessness that men experience at work can be partly compensated for by asserting power and authority in the home. Fourth, feminist sociologists point out that the patriarchal state, via policing and the courts, condones domestic violence in the home by failing to take the problem seriously.

In contrast, New Right thinkers believe the family is dysfunctional because of the emotional side effects of divorce on children and because the 'broken' one-parent family that results is producing delinquent children. Furthermore, some families according to Palmer are failing to socialise their children properly. Their children spend too much time watching television or on the internet and consequently children are increasingly selfish and antisocial in attitude.

It therefore cannot be assumed that the family is always positive for society. It is for most but for others it can be a nightmare.

e The student demonstrates an excellent knowledge and understanding of a range of relevant sociological theory and evidence, which is generally accurate and detailed. There is a clear line of reasoning and the material is focused on addressing the question. Analysis and evaluation are sustained by the student examining both the functionalist and New Right positions as a counterweight to the feminist perspective. This student is awarded full marks for all three skills (8 + 4 + 4). **16/16 marks awarded.**

6   Marxists believe that a wealthy minority — the capitalist class or bourgeoisie — monopolises wealth, income and power in capitalist societies like the UK by exploiting the labour-power of another larger class — the working class. However, Marxists argue that this capitalist class has constructed a superstructure of social institutions whose function is to transmit capitalist ideology to convince members of society that capitalism is just and fair. According to Marxists, the family is part of this ideological superstructure and its main role, therefore, is to serve the interests of capitalism by covering up or justifying inequality and exploitation.

e This an excellent introduction, which succinctly summarises the Marxist critique of capitalism and outlines the family's role as part of the superstructure. There is also good use of sociological concepts such as ideology.

Marxists such as Zaretsky claim that the nuclear family has three broad ideological functions which benefit the capitalist class at the expense of the working class. First, the family socialises children into capitalist values such as obedience and respect for authority and hierarchy. Such socialisation encourages working-class children and adults to be uncritical conformists who accept their unequal lot and low socioeconomic status in the capitalist system without question and to see inequality as normal and natural.

Second, Zaretsky argues that the nuclear family encourages the working class to focus on the home and family life, thereby diverting workers' attention and complaints and anger from the hardship and exploitation of the workplace. The family and the home function to help workers forget about how much they hate their jobs. Workers with families and children are less likely to go on strike and challenge inequality or the way capitalism is organised.

Third, the nuclear family is also an important market for consumer goods. The role of the mass media, according to Marxists, is to encourage the family to focus on the consumption of material goods and therefore to increase the profits made by the capitalist class. Many of the things families are encouraged to buy are not essential — they are what Marcuse calls 'false needs'. Again, materialism and consumerism serve to distract members of society away from the real reasons for inequalities in income, wealth and power.

Marxist-feminist sociologists such as Benston also argue that the nuclear family serves the interests of capitalism. She believes that the family oppresses women and serves capitalism in three ways. First, women produce the future labour force free of charge; second, women maintain the health and efficiency of the current adult workforce through housework free of charge; and third Ansley argues that women soak up men's frustrations about their lack of power and satisfaction in the workplace through domestic violence.

ⓔ Zaretsky's and Benston's studies are given the attention that they deserve. The three functions are outlined in depth with illustrations that clearly show that this student understands the material.

However, this Marxist analysis has been criticised because it over-focuses on the functions of the family and ignores what actually occurs within families. For example, interactionists note that Marxists ignore how individuals interact within families. Marxism tends to present an over-socialised view of children in which they are pumped full of capitalist ideology. Marxism fails to see that family socialisation is often a two-way process between parents and children. Moreover, Marxists overemphasise the nuclear family and neglect family diversity. Marxist-feminist theory may now be a little dated because of the feminisation of the economy and workforce.

Furthermore, in contrast, functionalist sociologists view the nuclear family more positively than Marxists and claim that it performs crucial functions for society and its members. Hakim claims that Marxist-feminists fail to acknowledge that being a mother–housewife can be a deeply satisfying role. Functionalists such as Murdock and Parsons note that the nuclear family brings about important social processes such as social solidarity by, for example, offering mutual support and emotional satisfaction through marriage and having children. Parsons notes that the nuclear family is able to 'stabilise adult personalities' in a stressful impersonal world by providing love, security and comfort for its members. It is a haven in a heartless world. In addition, the nuclear family also brings about social order by socialising its members into the basic values and norms of society (value consensus), thereby producing good citizens who obey laws and respect others. In this sense, therefore, the nuclear family serves society in general rather than the narrow interests of capitalism.

Other sociologists especially Weber criticise Marxists for overemphasising the role of social class and underplaying the influence of culture, especially that relating to ethnicity and religion, which may also produce power inequalities within the family. Feminists argue that patriarchy is far more important than class in explaining women's experience within families. Postmodernists would criticise Marxism for over-focusing on the nuclear family and failing to consider the diversity of family and personal life options available today.

ⓔ The student demonstrates an excellent knowledge and understanding of a broad range of relevant sociological theory focused on Marxism but also functionalism, feminism, interactionism and postmodernism. Sociological studies are both accurately employed and full of illustrative detail. The student is focused throughout on examining Marxist theory. Evaluation is explicit and detailed. It covers a wide range of ground. The student is awarded full marks for all skills. **24/24 marks awarded.**

ⓔ **Total score for Section B: 52/52 marks**

ⓔ **Total score for Paper 1: 90/90 marks**

A-level question 3

Socialisation, culture and identity

1   **Explain, using examples, the concept of consumer culture.**   (6 marks)

e Make sure you use at least two examples to illustrate this concept.

Source A

Source B

The concept of culture refers to the way of life of a particular society. This way of life equips members of society with language, values, religious beliefs, customs and a shared sense of history and tradition. Cultural symbols such as flags bind people together as cultural communities.

2   **Using Sources A and B and your wider sociological knowledge, explain the concept of culture.**   (12 marks)

e Define culture and illustrate it using the materials in the sources. Give examples of values and norms, and different types of culture — high, popular and global.

3   **Outline and briefly evaluate the view that age plays a significant part in the construction of identity.**   (20 marks)

e Show how age identity is socially constructed across the different age groups.

Family and relationships

4 Outline two reasons for the increase in single-person households and illustrate your answer with examples.

(12 marks)

ⓔ Focus on two different types of single-person households.

5 Explain and briefly evaluate the effect of an ageing population on family life.

(16 marks)

ⓔ Explain why the UK has an ageing population before you discuss its effects on the family.

6 Assess the view that the nuclear family is in decline.

(24 marks)

ⓔ This is the New Right position so you will need to discuss marriage, cohabitation, divorce and single-parent families. Remember you do not have to agree with the sentiment in the essay title.

Student answer

1 The concept of consumer culture is a postmodernist concept. It refers to the idea that modern society has been transformed into what Steve Taylor calls 'an endless shopping mall' in which people have greater choice about what they consume. Postmodernists argue that identity is now shaped by consumerism rather than social factors such as social class, gender, ethnicity and religion. The postmodern identity is about style and the conspicuous consumption of status symbols such as designer labels.

Lury notes that consumer culture offers a wide choice of consumer goods to buy. Shopping is therefore likely to be a popular and major leisure pursuit. Consumerism in these societies is both physical in that people go to shops but also virtual as people consume via the internet. A consumer culture is often underpinned by economic globalisation as brands like Nike, McDonald's, Microsoft, Facebook and Coca-Cola become part of our consumerist lives.

ⓔ The concept of consumer culture is clearly defined and successfully illustrated with reference to sociological theory, studies and concepts. The sociological material is focused on adding depth and detail to an understanding of consumer culture. **6/6 marks awarded.**

---

2 As the text source says, culture refers to the way of life of a particular society. It is the way that populations of societies make sense of their daily lives. Most sociologists believe that culture, which according to the source is made up of language, values, religious beliefs, customs and a shared sense of history and tradition, is something which is learned from other members of a group or community, rather than being transmitted biologically or genetically.

Culture is something which is shared by members of a society. This can be illustrated by examining components of culture such as values. Values are widely accepted beliefs that something is worthwhile and desirable. For example, British society places a high value on human life, education, privacy, money, material things, democracy, free speech, family life, children etc. The picture source shows a member of an Ethiopian tribe. Although there may be some overlap between British values and Ethiopian values, it is highly likely that these tribesmen value things that the British might find strange and even deviant. Other aspects of culture include norms. These are the unwritten and usually unspoken rules of behaviour that exist for virtually every specific social situation, and consequently they govern every aspect of human behaviour. For example, norms govern the way we dress, the way we prepare food and how we eat that food, our toilet behaviour and so on. Again, these are relative to particular societies.

It is important to understand that culture is also made up of high culture (creative activities which are highly valued), folk culture (traditions passed down through the generations) and popular culture (the products of the entertainment industry). Moreover, most cultures are diverse in the sense that societies are made up of a range of subcultures based on ethnicity, religion, youth, sexuality and politics. All have their own distinct mini-cultures which exist alongside the main culture. Globalisation too contributes to culture and can even change it. For example, the Ethiopian tribesman is using a mobile phone — a symbol of economic globalisation.

🅔 The concept of culture is clearly defined and successfully illustrated with reference to concepts. The discussion of concepts such as values, norms, high culture, folk culture, cultural diversity and so on is detailed and displays excellent knowledge and understanding. Another valid way of approaching this question might be a discussion of how sociological theories such as functionalism, Marxism and postmodernism view culture. However, the student is awarded the full 4 marks because this version displays an excellent understanding and uses the source material in a perceptive way. All the material used is highly relevant and focused on a discussion of culture and therefore the student is awarded the full 8 marks for this skill too. **12/12 marks awarded.**

3   Age plays an important role in the construction of identity and different societies treat the same age groups in different ways. Age identity is therefore socially constructed. For example, in preindustrial societies there is often no such thing as adolescence or teenagers. In many tribal cultures, when a child reaches puberty they are subjected to a ritual called a 'rite of passage' in which they are instructed in how to be a man or a woman. Once the ritual is over, the child is regarded as an adult with the same responsibilities as other adults. Another way to illustrate the social construction of age is to examine how old age is interpreted in tribal societies compared with modern societies like the UK. In tribal societies, old age is associated with wisdom and power and consequently the elderly are revered.

ⓔ This is an excellent introduction, which compares traditional society with modern society in order to introduce the concept of social construction.

In modern UK society, elderly people are not revered. In fact, it can be argued that they are treated with disrespect and that they often experience prejudice and discrimination called ageism. This is because status in the UK depends on being in work. People in the UK have traditionally retired from work in their sixties. However, there may be negative consequences. Sociologists have observed that loss of work can result in a significant decline in self-esteem, social contacts with others and income, and produce poverty, loneliness and depression.

Johnson and Bytheway suggest ageism has three aspects. First, it is often institutionalised in organisational and legal practices, e.g. workers who are made redundant in their mid-40s may experience age barriers in finding new jobs. Second, stereotypical prejudices might be experienced. Pilcher notes that old people are often labelled in derogatory or condescending ways. She argues that such stereotypes tend to label old people as inferior. The mass media may also be guilty of such stereotyping in terms of advertising being aimed at products which help people avoid ageing and the lack of elderly people on television. Third, ageism can involve the assumption that elderly people are vulnerable and dependent on younger adults for care.

ⓔ The above section clearly demonstrates detailed knowledge and understanding about elderly identity in modern societies, using relevant sociological studies.

It is not just the elderly generation who find that their age is used to define them. In industrial societies, childhood too is socially constructed. Aries notes that until the 1870s the concept of a child having a specific childhood identity did not exist because children worked in mines, mills and factories and often died young. The notion of an innocent childhood focused on play and school in which children are protected from external threats is a recent invention according to Cunningham.

In modern society the identity of teenagers is often presented as a problem. Society in general tends to be very critical of teenagers and almost fearful of them. The emergence of a specific teenage subculture and lifestyle with specific tastes in music and fashion has generally been seen as a problem. Youth has often been demonised as folk devils by the mass media and moral panics have been constructed around young people's behaviour. Sociologists such as Thornton suggest that teenagers are more frequently condemned than praised by the mass media, e.g. media reports have implied that most young people are knife- or gun-wielding hoodies.

However, studies of young people suggest that the generation gap implied by moral panics is exaggerated. Very few young people get involved with deviant youth subcultures or crime. Most young people are generally conformist — they get on well with their parents and place a high value on getting married etc.

e The student demonstrates an excellent knowledge and understanding of a range of sociological material on age identity, which includes perceptive analysis of traditional societies, old age, childhood and adolescence. All of the sociological studies and evidence discussed are of relevance and focused on the question. Evaluation is perhaps a little underdeveloped. Aries, for example, has been criticised and some sociologists believe that the importance of moral panics has been overstated. However, the contrast between traditional and modern societies is evaluative, as is the final paragraph. The student is therefore awarded 7 marks for knowledge and understanding, 8 marks for application and 3 marks for analysis and evaluation. **18/20 marks awarded.**

e Total score for Section A: 36/38 marks

---

4   One reason for the increase in single-person households has been the ageing of the population, which has led to a significant increase in the number of elderly one-person households. In 2013 over 50% of one-person households were made up of the elderly. Most were women because, on average, women live longer than men and they tend to marry men older than themselves. There are three times as many widows as there are widowers. However, these figures may fall in the near future as there are signs that the extended family may be making a comeback especially among the middle classes.

Another reason for the growth in the number of single-person households is that professional women may be choosing the single life while they establish their career and standard of living. There is statistical evidence that such women are postponing getting married and having children. Moreover, such women may be part of the growing and increasingly acceptable lifestyle choice known as LAT or 'living apart together'. These are couples who regard themselves as firmly committed to each other but who have separate homes through choice or circumstance. Duncan et al. (2013) found that LATs are predominantly young. They found that LATs chose to live apart because they desired a certain amount of freedom and independence.

---

e Two reasons for the growth in single-person households are clearly identified and explained using accurate statistical evidence and sociological studies. Both explanations are well illustrated and the material used is focused on single-person households. There could be a case for suggesting that both explanations might benefit from some contextual information — for example, why young women are able to pursue careers or why the population is ageing — but what is included displays excellent understanding. The student is therefore awarded 7 marks for knowledge and understanding and 4 marks for application because all the material is consistently applied to single-person households. **11/12 marks awarded.**

5   The decline in the death rate, especially the infant mortality rate, and the increase in life expectancy have led to an ageing of the UK population. The average age of the population is getting higher, with a greater proportion of the population over retirement age, and decreasing numbers of children under 16. The decline in the birth rate means that fewer children are being born. People aged over 65 years will outnumber people aged under 16 in the next few years.

The ageing of the population has a number of effects on family life according to feminists such as Pilcher. There may be a growth in the number of extended families as adult children care and support elderly relatives who do not have the economic resources to go into private residential care homes. This is likely to have knock-on effects. First, Pilcher argues that it may increase the domestic burden on women who take most responsibility for caring in families. Second, it may result in financial hardship for the family because one partner, usually the female, may have to give up work in order to care full time for elderly relatives. Third, there may be emotional strain and overcrowding if an elderly and physically dependent relative moves in and this causes conflict between couples, and between parents and children. Fourth, caring for others can increase stress and consequently result in ill health for carers.

The ageing of the population has led to an increase in the number of one-person elderly households as a proportion of all households. Women aged 65 and over are more likely to live alone than men because of their superior life expectancy and because they tend to marry men older than themselves. Although older people are increasingly living alone, this does not mean that they are isolated. Evidence suggests that many of them have regular contact with extended kin. Foster studied an East End London community and found that adults chose to live only a few streets away from their parents and grandparents, and visited them regularly. Ross found that two-thirds of grandparents saw their grandchildren once a week. Many elderly relatives use new technology such as e-mail to keep in contact with their extended kin.

Brannen (2003) notes that the ageing of the population has led to the recent emergence of four-generation families — that is, families that include great-grandparents and great-grandchildren but fewer aunts, uncles and cousins. Brannen argues that beanpole families are advantageous because they result in more qualitative and enriching contact between grandparents and their grandchildren.

ℯ The student displays an excellent knowledge of the effects of an ageing population on family life and uses a creditable range of sociological sources and evidence to cover a good range of issues: the effect on families and especially women who care for the elderly, extended family life and beanpole families, although the latter requires a bit more detail. All material is relevant and focused on answering the question. Although there is no specific evaluation, there is an evaluative tone throughout — for example, 'although old people are living alone, this does not mean they are isolated'. The student is awarded 7 marks for knowledge, 4 marks for application and 3 marks for evaluation. **14/16 marks awarded.**

> **6** New Right writers such as Morgan are concerned about a number of trends which they see as causing a decline in the nuclear family, including divorce, the decline in marriage and the increasing popularity of cohabitation. They are also concerned about the rising number of one-parent families, which they see as responsible for rising crime and delinquency rates.

ⓔ It is always important to set the scene and to contextualise the debate. The student has rightly identified the New Right as the source of the view that the nuclear family is under attack and supposedly in decline. Note too that the introduction acts like a plan of action.

> However, critics of the New Right suggest that their anxieties are exaggerated. First, many sociologists, including functionalists and feminists, argue that high divorce rates indicate higher expectations of marriage — people are no longer willing to put up with unhappy empty-shell marriages as in the past. Thornes and Collard note that it is women who are most likely to initiate divorce. This is because their new-found economic independence allows them to demand more of men in marriage and to reject patriarchal inequalities of power. These observations are supported by the fact that more than 40% of all marriages are remarriages (in which one or both partners have been divorced).
>
> The New Right's attitude towards declining marriage is also questioned. The evidence suggests that people are delaying marriage rather than rejecting it. The facts state that most people still see marriage as a desirable life goal or gold standard of relationships and will marry at some point in their lives. There is some evidence that women in particular may be delaying marriage because they want to develop their careers and enjoy a period of independence. Wilkinson argues that young females no longer see marriage and children as their main goals as their mothers and grandmothers once did. Educational opportunities and the feminisation of the economy have resulted in young women weighing up the costs of marriage and having children against the benefits of a career and economic independence.
>
> The New Right idea that marriage is being replaced by cohabitation can also be questioned. Surveys indicate that few people see cohabitation as an alternative to marriage. Beaujohan's research clearly shows that most couples see it as a test of compatibility and therefore as a dress rehearsal for marriage. Moreover, cohabitation is a temporary phase — it lasts on average about 5 years, and often it is a practical way of organising a relationship while awaiting divorce. Furthermore, approximately 60% of cohabiting couples eventually marry.

ⓔ The student has intelligently followed the plan incorporated into the introduction and examined divorce followed by marriage followed by cohabitation. The student has recognised the need for sociological evidence, which is presented in the form of sociological studies throughout the response.

> Feminist sociologists are critical of New Right arguments about one-parent families too. First, they point out that teenage pregnancy is not a major social problem — only 3% of unmarried mothers are teenagers. The average age of a single mother in the UK is 34 according to the National Council for One-Parent Families. Popay argues that single parents are often scapegoated for inner-city crime and educational underachievement, when these problems are actually the result of factors such as unemployment and poverty. Phoenix and Cashmore argue that most one-parent families succeed at providing their children with a secure and supportive family life, despite problems such as poverty.

e Here we see an intelligent reference to the feminist defence, which makes three succinct criticisms of the New Right position on single-parent families.

> Postmodernists are critical of the New Right idea that the nuclear family is in decline. They point out that the nuclear family is going through a positive process of change which is producing a healthy diversity of family types. The choice such diversity offers individuals and society is generally beneficial because it promotes tolerance of alternative family types such as gay and lesbian families. Such choice is particularly good for women, who no longer have to be tied to a full-time mother–housewife role for the rest of their lives. For example, in postmodern society, about one-fifth of women are voluntarily choosing not to have children.
>
> However, postmodernists too might be guilty of overexaggeration because, as Chester points out, married couples are still the main type of partnership in the UK and nuclear families are still the most common type of family. Six in ten families are still headed by a married couple and statistics suggest that the majority of children will never experience their parents going through a divorce.

e This evaluative section introduces the notion of diversity as a positive development but also questions the original assertion in the essay title that the nuclear family is in decline.

e Overall, this response displays an excellent understanding of the debate about family decline. It is firmly grounded in theory, it cites a range of sociological studies and evidence that questions the view contained in the essay title, and analyses and evaluates consistently throughout the essay. The student is therefore awarded full marks for each skill. **24/24 marks awarded.**

e **Total score for Section B: 49/52 marks**

e **Total score for Paper 1: 85/90 marks**

1 The belief in privacy.

2 It is an achieved status.

3 They are our main source of information about the consumer choices available to us, globalisation and so on.

4 They lack language, social skills, empathy with others, knowledge of socially acceptable norms of behaviour and so on.

5 Functionalists believe that both the academic and the hidden curricula benefit pupils and society because they combine to produce good citizens and effective workers, while Marxists believe they combine to produce exploited workers and conformist citizens who rarely question inequality.

6 Ideology is supposed to produce conformity but Willis' lads are not conforming to school rules (and therefore the hidden curriculum).

7 The peer group is a positive experience in that it helps its members cope with adolescence and helps young people establish an identity. However, peer group pressure may lead to young people engaging in antisocial or criminal behaviour and bullying.

8 The courts may punish via community service, fines and prison. Some societies still have capital punishment.

9 Being sent to the naughty step, withdrawal of love and other privileges, being smacked, being 'grounded' and so on.

10 Age, social class and ethnicity are not chosen. Society already has preconceived ideas about them. Gender too is mainly passive — but people can sometimes change their gender identity, for example, transsexuals.

11 Because their identity is the product of two cultures which often subscribe to very different norms, values and traditions.

12 Literature and history teaching stress aspects of Welsh poets and Welsh history respectively. Sport, particularly rugby union, is also a powerful medium of national identity.

13 Sex refers to biological differences between males and females, while gender refers to how different societies view masculine and feminine behaviour.

14 Boys are more likely to physically bully their peers, while girls more often use social media to verbally bully.

15 The mother–housewife role.

16 Professionals, managers and white-collar workers.

17 Consumption of consumer goods and mass media.

18 The emergence of openly gay subcultures in British cities, the targeting of the pink pound by advertisers, the legalisation of gay civil marriage and the media acceptance of the lifestyle of gay celebrities.

19 A moral panic is a period or bout of social anxiety experienced by a large section of the population about a 'threat' to social order posed by a certain group or problem caused by exaggerated and sensationalist reporting by tabloid newspapers.

20 Ageism is a form of prejudice and discrimination which is practised against age groups, although it is most likely to be practised against elderly people.

21 There are a number of reasons: slum clearance in inner-city areas and the relocation of people to new towns and council estates; full employment and the welfare state; the reform of education in 1944; and the large numbers of women entering the workforce.

22 Liberal feminists argue that the role of women in families has dramatically improved as they have become joint breadwinners and now make an important contribution to family finances and living standards. Moreover, easy access to divorce means they can escape unhappy marriages.

23 It is supposedly under threat from social policies such as divorce, the legalisation of homosexuality and abortion, and the welfare state, cohabitation and the rise in the number of one-parent families.

24 Changes in the law, the liberalisation of social attitudes, the changing expectations of women and secularisation.

25 The feminisation of the economy and workforce, women's changing priorities, the availability of effective contraception and the declining influence of extended kin.

26 Better living standards, improvements in the quality of medical care and the welfare state have all contributed to increases in life expectancy, while a fall in both the birth rate and the fertility rate means fewer children are being born compared with the past.

27 Children of divorced parents often belong to two families — they may live with their mother but may also spend time with their father's post-divorce family set-up.

28 They have become more common because people are living longer, parents are choosing to have fewer children and there are reciprocal benefits in terms of childcare and care of elderly relatives.

29 Elderly widows and widowers, middle-aged male divorcees, young career women and those who are together but choose to live apart from each other (LATs).

30 Racism or hostility from one or both of the two cultural groups from which they originate and confusion over their social identity.

31 It is a type of nuclear family in which there is supposedly equality between the sexes with regard to the distribution of domestic work, decision making and so on.

32 The partnership penalty suggests that when men and women move in together and/or get married the woman ends up doing more housework than when she was single. Chore wars refers to conflicts that occur because the female feels the male is not doing enough housework or childcare.

33 Murder, domestic violence and the different types of child abuse.